# FRIENDSHIP
*and*
# WAYS *to* TRUTH

# FRIENDSHIP
## *and*
# WAYS *to* TRUTH

David B. Burrell, C.S.C.

UNIVERSITY OF NOTRE DAME PRESS
Notre Dame, Indiana

© 2000 by
University of Notre Dame Press
Notre Dame, Indiana 46556
All Rights Reserved
http://www.undpress.nd.edu

Manufactured in the United States of America


*Library of Congress Cataloging-in-Publication Data*
Burrell, David B.
Friendship and ways to truth / David B. Burrell.
p.   cm.
ISBN 0-268-02859-1 (alk. paper)
1. Friendship—Religious aspects—Christianity.
2. Christianity and other religions.   I. Title.
BV4647.F7 B87   2000
241'.6762—dc21        00-008603

∞ *This book is printed on acid-free paper.*

*In gratitude*

✨    *for friends on the journey*    ✨

*to truth*

# Contents

# Acknowledgments

An earlier version of chapter 3 appeared in *Irish Theological Quarterly* 62 (1996/97): 185–99, and the original version of chapter 4 appeared in *The Changing Face of Friendship,* ed. Leroy Rouner (Notre Dame, Ind.: University of Notre Dame Press, 1994). I am immensely grateful for the care which Rebecca DeBoer exhibited in copyediting my original text.

# Friendship, Community, Tradition

"The Lord said to Abram: 'Leave your country, your kindred and your father's house for a country which I shall show you. . . .' So Abram went as the Lord told him . . ." (Gen 12:1,4). What is the relation between experience and truth in this encounter? God spoke to him; Abram did what he was asked to do. Simple enough, and logically airtight: as Wittgenstein remarks, "'You can't hear God speaking to someone else, you can hear him only if you are being addressed'. That is a grammatical remark."[1] And, we should add, perspicuously so; there are no doubts about who is speaking or about the import of the request—if it be a request and not an order. But that is the marvel about scripture, be it Bible or Qur'an: God's speaking is always perspicuous; even the dreams attested are clearly from the Lord. Self-validating, we might say, where the *self* in question is the divine word who creates and sustains us. No way out of that circle; one can only be admitted into it![2]

Yet any other situation—and need we be reminded that any situation we may experience is *other* than these!—confronts us with an utterly ambiguous relation between experience and truth. We are normally compelled to ask of most assertions and all events: what does that mean? How am I to read my friend's death? What consequences ought it have for me? Truth is eminently personal yet correlatively cosmic, so "true for me" is ungrammatical. The most congenial images that come to mind are those of *fit* or of *recognition*. But there are also Jesus' words: "the truth shall make you free," said by the one who dares to claim: "I am the way, the truth, and the life; follow me!" Presumably *to* the truth, yet the way to the truth can also be said to be the *true* (or *straight*) path. And what Jesus' words presume, without asserting, is that this *way* will be constituted by personal encounters. The way to truth will entail meeting others and journeying with them. For whatever truth is, it is not something we start with but something we discover. We might say, mimicking Wittgenstein, if truth is to be had, it will only be had in a tradition, within a community, in the company of friends. For each of these terms implies the other: tradition without a sustaining and connecting community is nothing but past history; and we are formed into communities by the cross-hatching of friendships, and especially of friends bound together by their shared faith in a communal goal. So the relation of student to teacher becomes one of fellow travelers on a journey, even when that encounter takes place across several centuries.

We may even say that history comes alive in and through friendships. Certainly what is most significant in the relationship between God and Abraham is its history; in this case, a history turned into a legacy inherited directly by two peoples, Jews and Arabs, and adopted by two religious families, Christians and Muslims. Scriptural reference to Abraham as a "friend of God" (James 2:23, citing Isaiah 41:8) offers the ground for his descendants being called "God's people," and becomes the cachet allowing Christians and Muslims to appropriate that title as well. Yet that proximity leads directly to the excoriation of Ezekiel 16; histories at once bind and empower, and friendships both require and acquire a history, if they are to live up to their promise. (I was reminded of that recently by receiving from my friend Stanley Hauerwas a copy of his contribution to a colloquium which the theology faculty at Notre Dame held fifteen years ago to ease me out of being their chairman, an exploration entitled: "Friendship: An Exercise in Theological Understanding.") 'Exercise' turns out to be the operative word in that title, as evincing a "willingness to place our life and needs in the hands of another." And that takes time, as Aristotle has reminded us; time and testing circumstances which can never be foreseen.

Jesus' "follow me" invites one to walk with him, and so enter into a shared history. Yet no one but Jesus could say "follow me"; we can at best say, "let us follow this path," where the path is said to lead to truth. In that sense, neither person is following the other but both are letting themselves be drawn by what they discern—individually and together—to be the *true* or *straight* path which will lead each of them to the truth of their lives. Yet even to speak such language, we are being reminded today, requires that we share a source and a goal. For there can be no truth without creation, as George Steiner has so forcibly argued in his *Real Presences*.[3] For the ancients, the alternative was emanation from the One, so that Augustine was faced with a decision which seems to us bizarre: to become a Christian or a Platonist! Yet that alternative cannot be a real one in a "postmodern" world; "the One" detached from a creator can be nothing more than a vain conceptual ideal, which probably marks an intellectual advance. For the *truth* we could recognize, if we can recognize any at all, has to be a personal source which becomes at once our goal, reinforcing the image of the "true path" demanding a personal encounter. And where that truth is at once our source and goal, it also calls us to become someone: notably, the self we are called to become by virtue of our originating relation with that truth, which thereby inscribes us with a destiny. If that term has frightening connotations, as it doubtless will, we can attenuate them by reminding ourselves that this truth is eminently *personal* in character, so however we might conceive our *destiny*, it need not be fatalistic.

With creation, however, the way forward is the way back. As Eliot reminded us: "What we call the beginning is often the end / And to make an end is to make a beginning. / The end is where we start from" ("Little Gidding," lines 114–16). But how can we find the way back in order to locate the way forward? Jesus' response is straightforward enough: "Follow me; . . . I am the way, the truth, and the light." Yet our connection with Jesus must be through his disciples; the way of *mimesis* lies with friends who are friends "in Christ." Here is where we can identify the role which community and tradition play in facilitating our finding the way back and the way forward. Alasdair MacIntyre has reminded us that we have no choice about this; those who pretend to operate outside any tradition by claiming the ground of rational discourse are themselves guided by the tradition called "liberalism."[4] Another way of putting the matter is to insist that Newman has won; that any argument and all discourse proceed from implicitly held perspectives which can be formulated as premises, and which themselves are not up for scrutiny.[5]

We have no choice about this, although we do have a choice about a community and a tradition, and plenty of freedom in negotiating our mode of insertion in both. In fact, we can even identify the criteria for a viable tradition in terms of its depth and amplitude, as evidenced in its capacity of self-criticism—the criterion advanced by MacIntyre. This seems to happen quite naturally, as we find ourselves attracted to another way of thinking about things, or even of worshipping God, and are subsequently able (or not) to discover what attracted us elsewhere in hitherto unplumbed reaches of our own tradition. If we cannot, then we may be constrained to switch allegiances; those traditions which keep managing to accommodate our wandering spirit then become viable traditions, or "major religions." Yet it is inevitably friends who make it possible for us to bond with a community or a tradition, helping us by their example to discover ways in which we can participate in them individually and fruitfully. For according to an Aristotelian view of friendship, by contrast with a more romantic one, we become friends to the extent that we share in an attracting and encompassing goal or good. Interestingly enough, however, such a sharing has more to do with intention than with agreement. Indeed, as a friendship unfolds, it offers the paradigm for sustaining a relationship beyond disagreements—even "all the way down," so long as we recognize that there are depths beyond the reaches of reason itself, and we continue to journey into these together.[6]

These reflective essays explore the role friends play in our coming to the truth, beginning with a personal account of a friendship recently completed in its earthly phase. The next essay assesses a friendship of a more philosophical sort, engaging Plato and Augustine to show how Diogenes Allen and I have come mutually to discover just how indispensable are "spiritual exercises" to that "knowing-by-faith" which marks our critical appropriation of truth. The third set of reflections was occasioned by an invitation from a friend, Enda McDonagh, to participate in the bicentenary of Saint Patrick's College in Maynooth (Eire). Acknowledging three personal companions along the way— Bernard Lonergan, Stanley Hauerwas, and Aurelius Augustine— I explore the ways friends can open our hearts and minds to interfaith dialogue, moving it beyond the specter of "relativism" to a fruitful stage of "mutual illumination." The fourth chapter allows us to engage al-Ghazali and Thomas Aquinas in dialogue, to show how two exemplary thinkers from the Muslim and Christian traditions offer "mutually illuminating" perspectives to extend the reach of friendship to embrace the creator. The final chapter moves us explicitly to understanding divinity and suggests that friendship offers us indispensable help to "go on" in the face of the radical unknowing which must characterize philosophical theology. Indeed, without those spiritual exercises which link friends embarked on an intellectual journey, the crucial distinction between creator and creatures will inevitably be obscured by philosophers striving to accommodate divinity to their established categories. The only possible result, it is argued, will be idolatry. Thus the contribution which friendship can make to intellectual inquiry becomes invaluable, especially in those regions which continue to defy proper conceptualization.

## Notes

1. *Zettel,* ed. and trans. G. E. M. Anscombe (Berkeley: University of California Press, 1967), #717.

2. See the fascinating essay by Bruce Marshall, "What Is Truth?" *Pro Ecclesia* 4 (1995): 404–30, for a penetrating study of Christ as "the Truth" and its implication for inquiry.

3. *Real Presences* (London: Faber and Faber, 1989).

4. *Whose Justice? Which Rationality?* (Notre Dame, Ind.: University of Notre Dame Press, 1988), chap. 17: "Liberalism Transformed into a Tradition."

5. John Henry Newman, *An Essay in Aid of a Grammar of Assent* (Notre Dame, Ind.: University of Notre Dame Press, 1978), with a preface by Nicholas Lash outlining his pattern of "retrospective verification." For an illuminating journey through all of this, see Joseph Dunne, *Back to the Rough Ground* (Notre Dame, Ind.: University of Notre Dame Press, 1993), chap. 1: "J. H. Newman's Appeal to Phronesis in *A Grammar of Assent.*"

6. At the close of his final argument in the *Phaedo,* and just before the concluding myth, Socrates advises Simmias: "what you say is right, so the initial hypotheses, even if they're acceptable to you people, should still be examined more clearly: If you analyze them adequately, you will, I believe, follow the argument to the furthest point to which a human being can follow it up; and if you get that clear, you'll seek nothing further" (107b5–10).

# Grieving the Death of a Friend

Eskimos are said to have countless words to express what we simply call 'snow', for they relate to it as the atmosphere surrounding their very life. We certainly need a plethora of words for the intimate and variegated process we call 'grieving', for not only does each of us go through it differently, but the way we undergo it is colored by the relationships involved and certainly by the manner of our friend's dying. Friendships also vary in ways well worth describing, as we shall see; one person's account of grieving a friend's death will help another only if that account is given in sharp relief, so that others will be able to discern what is similar from what is different in their respective situations. Such comparisons help us more than we can say; often the differences are even more illuminating than the similarities. For one telling example, I would be at a loss to understand how to grieve the sudden death of a close friend, to say nothing—nothing at all!—about a friend's taking his or her own life. My own experience, as we shall see, is far less traumatic than either of those, yet describing it in its very particularity may allow others to do the same for their own grieving. One last prefatory note: my language will try to respect the fact that grieving, like friendship and nearly everything significant in our lives, is not something we do; it is something we undergo. Once we realize that the root for our word 'suffering' is the same as 'undergoing', we have taken a step towards undermining the modern presumption that suffering is the worst of all evils.

That presumption is connected, of course, with its comple-ment: that the best situation is one in which we are "in control," which leaves us with nothing more than the banal language of "dealing with" or "coping" to confront events like the death of a friend. It is a mark of the wisdom born of suffering when we are able to parry attempts to comfort us cast in those terms with a straightforward: "I'm neither 'dealing with it' nor am I 'coping', thank you. I'm just letting it sink in; suffering it, you might say!" So the friendship that has been ours is something that neither of us did; it gradually insinuated itself into our lives, shaping them into what they have become. That process entailed our doing a number of things, of course, but the reality itself was none of our doing. Neither is grieving, even though countless persons will suggest things that we ought to do, some of them extremely useful. Yet these are at best aids to a process that we can only suffer, undergo; undergoing it is precisely what we are called to do in response to the gift of friendship. This new grammar—an ancient one, of course, yet new to moderns—suggests the di-rection our reflections will take: as friendship is a gift we have learned to receive and be immensely grateful for, so we learn through it—and through its ostensible loss—that life itself is a gift, whose loss leaves a space as ample, or as restricted, as our capacity to have received it. Indeed, *capacity* becomes the clue we shall be following: friendship, death, and grieving all effect capacities in us; it is out of those spaces that we learn how to live.

Ours was a friendship between two men; the friendship of David and Jonathan offers the biblical archetype. John and I were brothers in a brotherhood as old as western monasticism, yet as variegated as modern religious communities can be. Ours is one of those, barely 150 years old; the initials after our names, 'C.S.C.', signify 'Congregatio a Sancta Cruce' or 'Congregation of Holy Cross'. Normally friendships in religious communities can be traced to the years of formation, beginning with novitiate, when a heterogeneous group of individuals from diverse family backgrounds are taught the rigors of living together. That's all there is to it, really: learning to live together! The teaching consists of a life in common: of prayer punctuated by studies and sports, with some excelling in one or the other of the latter, and each learning to counter the inbuilt ethos of the playground with strange gospel injunctions against pressing one's advantage. Prayer is of course at once familiar and strange to all of us, and the common frame masked what would become telling individual differences in this crucial component of our lives. Prayer would become the most individual feature of each of our lives, with those who became attuned to its personal rhythms growing apace. In retrospect, it can be said that John's and my friendship turned on prayer, on the need each of us felt to discover it afresh in our lives as they unfolded—but that is to get ahead of the story.

We had not known each other during formation; he was ordained before me and had completed his studies for ordination in Washington, D.C., while I had been sent to Rome. We were thrown together in New Haven, as I began doctoral studies in philosophy and he continued work in English, after receiving an

M.A. from Cambridge, where he had studied under F. R. Leavis. We did not take to each other at first; he seemed to know it all, with Leavis's judgment final on anything of importance, and I doubtless had to flout my "superior" intelligence—typical male posturing, one might say. Yet we grew to respect one another, taking frequent walks after supper and playing squash together. Our friends moved in different circles, defined by our different course of studies, yet slowly a bonding took place that imperceptibly shaped our respective views of graduate studies and our shared religious life. We journeyed infrequently for soirées to a nearby house of our community, where I made the acquaintance of some of his contemporaries whom I had not known previously, and enjoyed their repartee even if I could never keep up with their drinking. But that meant that John always had someone to drive us home, another small mark of a growing friendship! During our first year we shared chaplaincy responsibilities to our Holy Cross brothers teaching in a high school in West Haven, which meant rising early enough to preside at 6:30 mass each weekday morning, while one of us helped in the local parish on weekends, with a splendid pastor who asked very little but appreciated whatever we did.

John heartily resented the "scholarly" approach to the study of English at Yale; it stood in hefty contrast with the more substantive approach of Leavis at Cambridge, which had appealed to his innate penchant for judgment. He once remarked, as I alighted from my bike with a simple book bag, that "you philosophers only need a pencil while we scholars need a dump truck." The following year was my turn to hole up in the Sterling Library drafting a dissertation. I was now living at the Catholic chaplaincy and assisting at a black parish on Sundays, while John adopted an Italian outstation of the local parish as his weekend ministry, with fledgling parish council meetings at the local Hofbrau. We saw less of each other that year, but played squash regularly and shared the travails of graduate study. Turning thirty in the 1960s, I was anxious to get on with a real life, so I returned with a completed draft of my thesis to teaching at Notre Dame, leaving John to continue the rigors of scholarly life for another two years. We were reunited on his return to Notre Dame in the joint venture of directing a student residence with our mutual friend and confrere, Ernie Bartell, only to be faced soon with the crisis which Vietnam posed for young men of that generation. Thus began our baptism of fire: undertaking a ministry which put us at odds with university decorum, the convictions of a number of our confreres, and inevitably the local FBI, yet all in response to the demands of the times and of the students whom we were teaching. We also managed to help initiate a freshman humanities program which epitomized education in the classics according to Leavis, and by the fall of 1969 the three of us were drawn to concelebrate a campus-wide moratorium mass called to hasten the end of American involvement in Vietnam.

All of this activity took its toll, however, and a semester sabbatical gave the time and space for reflection. Its improbable location was Dallas, because Perkins School of Theology (at Southern Methodist University) had offered me an apartment for my services as "resident Catholic scholar," and John could join me to try to bring his lingering dissertation to completion. The conversations we had in the interstices marked that year for both of us, conversations about prayer, love and celibacy, and other inevitable topics of the times. John had begun to work with a wise woman, Helen Luke, who thus introduced both of us to Jung; we learned to read the scriptures in a fresh way,

informed by John's literary background and our growing at-
tunement to a symbolic reading of revelation. John was later to
make a point of thanking me for displaying a fidelity to morning
meditation during those months together, something which
he took up with characteristic tenacity once he had negotiated
the life-shaping step of joining AA over Easter of our spring in
Dallas. The further blessing of that time apart was his mo-
mentous decision *not* to finish the thesis, to resign from the
faculty at Notre Dame, and remove himself to Window Rock,
Arizona, to teach Navajo children—the result of an American
Indian child beckoning in a decisive dream. The two years spent
there were to corroborate his symbolic reading of scripture in an
atmosphere favoring such interior understandings; we managed
to spend a Holy Week together at the monastery of Christ in the
Desert (near Abiquiu, New Mexico), which allowed me to feel
how much the Southwest and Navajo culture had penetrated his
spiritual grasp of nearly everything.

Before long John was invited by his religious community to
serve in ministry to us, first as local superior at Notre Dame, then
as assistant provincial, and finally as director of formation for
young men studying for priesthood—a total of sixteen years in
all. Such ministry is more taxing than it appears, for it means responding to one's confreres' call to remind us of what we have
promised in our vows—yet no one relishes being reminded
of that! During those years (1974–1990) we took up two practices which would shape our respective lives: weekly overnight
getaways to our community house on Lake Michigan, and an-
nual directed retreats over Christmas break. These were supple-
mented, when possible, by a reading/hiking interlude in some
secluded place just after classes were over in the spring, for
even if John was not directly involved in academic life, our lives

were inevitably measured out in semesters. The directed retreats proved the key to everything else, for they ensured that the symbolic reading of the scriptures, learned from Jung, would be integrated into a practice of prayer initiated by Ignatius and quite recently retrieved by Jesuits for the whole church. We migrated south together in early January, soon discovering two or three places (with directors) which became dear to us, notably Knobs Haven in Nerinx, Kentucky, and the Desert House of Prayer in Tucson, Arizona. The discipline of centering prayer, learned assiduously on a directed retreat, managed to perdure during the ensuing year for us, and the weekly times together let us take stock of these and other matters so essential to men and women in religious life, but which men, at least, often find quite difficult to broach to one another.

It was in that context of sharing what is most important in our lives, indeed when I was deep into my own need to share the loss by suicide of a Chinese co-worker and "daughter"—as I had come to appreciate what our relationship had become—that John had to inform me of an imminent biopsy for a curious lump he had discovered in his neck when inadvertently stroking it while reading. The diagnosis came shortly: untreatable liver cancer of unknown origin, with a six-month prognosis. Indeed, a final meeting with Helen Luke (who was to die a month later at the age of ninety) helped him to see how his own dreams had been trying to alert him to this over the past couple of months. Yet he was able to complete his teaching of a sophomore humanities seminar that fall before a clotting situation brought on by liver malfunction prompted him to move to our medical facility at Notre Dame. There began his final journey, one that he consciously undertook and in which he allowed us to accompany him. We had planned to make our retreat that January at the Desert House of Prayer, but the clotting restricted John's travel, so we made it (together with a Holy Cross sister friend, Elena Malits) at Holy Cross house where John was staying. We also continued our weekly overnights at our lake house well into March. On Ash Wednesday John composed a letter to his numerous friends, indicating that he was at peace, assured that the Lord had nothing more for him to do but this, and asking our prayers that he complete the journey well. He even expressed relief that he did not have to learn the computer after all—a characteristic light touch that had become John over the years.

We did our best to walk with him during those months of Lent, as he undertook one final thing after another, presiding at our Wednesday community eucharist as well as with the graduate students on Sunday evening, where he served as chaplain. The last was an open AA meeting, where he recapitulated the twenty-six years since that Easter in Dallas, leaving us all with the memorable phrase: "we can live out our lives either in resentment or in gratitude—there is no middle ground—and I have been made immensely grateful." During Holy Week I made the weekly journey to our lake house alone, as John's situation precluded his leaving the medical facility. Looking out over Lake Michigan the next morning, I asked myself why I should go on living. He had made it as easy as possible for his friends to walk with him, but what were we to do at the precipice? No answer came, but the question posed assured me that I could not supply an answer myself; it would have to come to me. That very evening I was called to be with him, and his close friends gathered for the vigil which coincided with the church's triduum—Holy Thursday, Good Friday, and Holy Saturday. He drifted in and out of consciousness, yet remained focused on those around him, responding to his dearest friend when she

asked him, "what do you want?" that he wanted to "go home."
And that he did, at noon on Easter Sunday, the deep toll of the
requiem intermingled with the carillon of Alleluias proper to the
liturgy of resurrection.

What can we learn from this? What have I learned from
this journey together to a decisive end? That friendship cannot
end; that (as Aristotle noted so presciently) "one stands in the
same relation to his friend as to himself" (*Nicomachean Ethics* 9.12,
1171b33). So we can become transformed vicariously in the
transformation of those whose lives have become intertwined
with ours. Into the emptiness can come an abiding gratitude for
a friendship so precious. Can that be grieving? I believe so, for it
forcibly reminds us that we cannot make it on our own, which
has to be the lasting legacy of a profound friendship, and the enduring face of a friend—lost yet never to be lost. In this way we
can celebrate how each of us can present to another the face
of "the good"—not, certainly, because we ourselves can be said
to embody that good, but because we reflect how we have
learned to journey towards it, together.

## 2

# *Friends in Conversation*
## *The Language and Practice of Faith*

It is a commonplace how easily friends can resume conversations just where they left them years ago; such has always been the case between me and Diogenes Allen. Tracing the parallel and convergent paths on which our inquiry has led us can illustrate how friendship and inquiry mutually sustain each other. Our years of graduate study date from a period when language reigned, especially in Oxford, where Dick was a Rhodes scholar. Philosophers even classified themselves as "ordinary language" philosophers, meaning that they resolved to take their cues and even find their operative distinctions imbedded in the rich texture of ordinary discourse. The inspiration, of course, was Ludwig Wittgenstein of the *Philosophical Investigations,* while the foil was the dream of an ideal or perfect language which Wittgenstein himself had earlier essayed in his *Tractatus Logico-Philosophicus.* In retrospect, we can see clearly that the impetus away from an ideal language signaled the end of an adequate separation of theoretical from practical understanding, of philosophy as pure discourse (replete with a technical vocabulary) from the practices required to employ "ordinary language" accurately and fruitfully. For language is ordinarily learned as a way of negotiating our world, with its accuracy tested as it helps us to do that more successfully. Yet the criteria for successfully negotiating a world gain in complexity as that world unfolds from one focused on personal satisfaction to one focused on general well-being, indeed, on the well-being of the universe. What sort of demands does that put on our use of language?

It demands an awareness, I shall suggest, that our speech will never quite be adequate to our quest for understanding; that our analysis of a situation, as we attempt to negotiate it properly, will inevitably leave something unconsidered. This is palpably the case in human affairs, where our initial orienting judgments tend to reduce another person to two dimensions, and so will betray us unless we leave them open to generous revision. That process is tantamount to "getting to know someone," where the knowledge in question requires vigilant efforts to interpret and reinterpret their actions. Often this proves fruitless, of course, or there is little incentive to keep up the effort it takes, but when something about that person lures us on further, as the prospect of authentic friendship begins to open, we are prodded to a more and more careful use of language. And we do so not simply to avoid offending someone about whom we have come to care, but as a way of enlisting our friend's services to better assess the world we share. For authentic friendship, as Aristotle so clearly noted, opens persons beyond "our relationship" to what he summarily called "the good"; that is, to seeking a proper relationship to the universe itself.

This dynamic has fueled Dick Allen's treatment of "the reasonableness of faith" from the beginning: language is crucial yet remains a vehicle for understanding, an understanding to which we are mysteriously called in our effort to negotiate a world which becomes ever more fascinating.[1] The effort which that quest calls forth will be concentrated on accurate and fruitful expression—for oneself and for others—but what animates that expression always exceeds what we can say. This phenomenon reminds us how discourse is constantly reaching beyond itself, at the service of something else—hence the guiding image of conversation between friends. For conversation imbeds discourse in an interpersonal context, while friendship (à la Aristotle) requires that interpersonal contexts be imbedded in something larger than the personal if they are to lead us where authentic friendship promises to lead. Here our own experience readily confirms the contention of Aristotle: friendship requires mutual trust to unfold, yet even that mutuality demands more than two persons can muster; for no one is immune to those power games which erode trust, or even a betrayal which destroys it. There must be something (or someone) more in which (or in whom) we may put our trust, if the interpersonal friendship is to develop into what it promises. Here is where life pushes us beyond calculation to trust, beyond reason to faith. Yet that step beyond, as we have seen, is precisely what the logic of love demands of us.

Faith must in that sense be reasonable, yet the reasonableness is not an abstract one, nor a fruitless one of calculating my advantage, but rather one that is demanded by conversation among friends. For nothing but faith can provide a context rich enough to offset the inevitable tendency of relationships to serve an "égoisme à deux," the tendency which Jews identify as the *yetzer ra,* Christians as "original sin," and Muslims as the state of ignorance (*jâhiliyya*). Why so? One could amass authorities here like Michel Foucault, whose relentless reminders of the multiple

21

ways in which discourse serves power have put us acutely on guard against "civility" or "sweet reasonableness." Yet as pervasive as power may be, it cannot be the last word, as the metaphysical lure of friendship never ceases to remind us, and as the struggle to keep friendship authentic confirms in us. It can even become increasingly difficult to speak the truth, as and when we see it, to someone with whom our life is intertwined, as spouses know so well. Yet the demand to do so, and to have our perspective corrected or enhanced, never ceases. We can never claim to "have the truth," to fully know another, since our articulations of what we think to be the case are always up for revision. Nor is this assertion simply asserted, for its truth emerges from friendship itself, which proves to be a relationship we can never cease pursuing if we are to lay claim to it.

Paradoxes like these lace our lives and require an increasing sensitivity to the language we use and the way we use it. This sensitivity is not necessarily a technical proficiency in specialized discourse, but rather an acquired expertise in knowing how to use properly terms which are common enough yet defy definition—like 'love' or 'friendship'. It is in the use of such terms that theory and practice intertwine to produce the kind of understanding that is proper to matters of faith and interpersonal relations. The practices in question, as we have seen, will embrace individual persons in relationship, introducing them into a community of interaction. And communities have histories, so what results is tradition. In this organic way, the internal linkage between tradition, community, faith, and practices begins to emerge as we probe the very conditions for a fruitful, non-exploitative relationship, epitomized by a conversation among friends. Some of these practices will inevitably be ritualized, as exchanges of affection are among friends, and the more so as the friend's presence is wanting—letters or phone calls are always more than exchanges of information. Moreover, practices among friends will take a shape provided by the context which embraces them, and so something of the faith that sustains their friendship will be detectable in the grammar of such practices. Here is where prayer and liturgical ritual enter for those whose faith is an explicit one, yet analogues will doubtless be sought and found by persons open to the dynamic of friendship without an explicit religious faith.

The extensive work of Pierre Hadot has come to the attention of the English-speaking world in recent years, releasing one to speak of "spiritual exercises" as an integral part of doing philosophy. Indeed, as Arnold Davidson cites Hadot in an introductory essay to an astute collection of his articles, "the written philosophical work [of Aristotle and of Plotinus], precisely because it is a direct or indirect echo of oral teaching, now appears to us as a *set of exercises,* intended to make one practice a method, rather than as a doctrinal exposition."[2] In other words, a restricted conception of philosophy as discourse has allowed us to overlook the degree of "pragmatic consistency" which their philosophical endeavors called for. The Socrates of Plato's dialogues has long offered the paradigm example of such an ideal, but the very expository form of Aristotle's prose could easily mislead teachers and students alike to conjecture that a new ideal of philosophical discourse was already being proposed in Aristotle's approach to doing philosophy. It has been Hadot's genius to identify the integral role of practices in late antiquity as well, notably in the work of Plotinus.[3]

Modern readers of Augustine's *Confessions* could understandably have been puzzled when the young man in search of truth felt constrained to decide between "the Platonists" and "the

Christians" (notably in book 7), for most of us could identify not a few "Christian Platonists." Yet such identifications in our time usually name "philosophical positions" (or in Hadot's terms, "doctrinal expositions"), whereas in Augustine's time one was speaking of communities of discourse with specified *exercises* of membership, designed to bring out the existential consequences of philosophical thought and conversation. Discourse was decidedly at the service of forming persons of a particular sort, whose very way of life would testify to the truth of the discourse.[4] It is that conception of philosophy, I would suggest, which has animated Diogenes Allen's work from the outset. In this sense, Pierre Hadot's historical and exegetical inquiries have served to contextualize a particular picture of "philosophy as discourse," notably written discourse, which proved so congenial to modernity, thus paving the way for the fresh optic called "postmodern."

What was it that led Diogenes Allen in that direction from the 1950s onward? Unable to penetrate my friend's mind, I can only essay an answer to that question by reflecting on the characteristics of my work which have consistently intersected with his, and indeed which led to our friendship early on. In 1975 I published a series of essays on classical and modern philosophers—from Augustine to Jung—entitled *Exercises in Religious Understanding*. The goal was less expository and more an invitation to readers to apprentice themselves to each of these thinkers, employing an accessible text from each, as they grappled with questions as real to us as to them. The writing itself emerged from teaching introductory philosophy using key texts from Augustine, Anselm, Aquinas, and Kierkegaard. (The essay on Jung's *Memories, Dreams, Reflections* was a more personal addition, intended to redirect some egregious misreadings of his work.) The inspiration of my teaching and writing had been Bernard Lonergan's reflections on hermeneutics, directing contemporary readers of ancient writers to identify the questions to which these writers' arguments were directed. This disarmingly simple approach enables readers to connect with texts and authors from the past so as to allow their work to illuminate the way in which contemporary readers would pose these questions, as well as cast light on current ways of answering them. It is ever the questions which engage us, and one can learn rather quickly to distinguish the terms which are translatable from those which are not.

Directions of this sort serve to remind teachers that the "history of philosophy" can be more philosophy than history, and to direct students beyond the goal of mastering a particular thinker's *position* on something—or what is far worse, the teacher's "position" on the particular thinker's "position"—to the goal of learning to negotiate the question itself from the way in which an acknowledged master has done so. That is what apprenticing amounts to: watching a master do what I want to learn to do myself. There can never be a direct transfer of skill; the primary agent must be the student's own capacities. But that should be the lesson of any course in philosophy; text and teacher are both, at best, "inadequate secondary causes."[5] It may also be true, of course, that such a view of philosophy would come most naturally to someone engaged in philosophical theology, where the articulations will be *ex professo* inadequate. Here we can extend Hadot's thesis to appreciate the transformation worked in doing philosophy from ancient to medieval times, where the exercises associated with conceptual clarification are explicitly at the service of a mode of understanding which attempts to articulate things quite beyond our human ken. As Aquinas put it, in a formulation anticipating Kant, the "object proper to human understanding is the quiddity of material things."[6]

But why should attempts to transcend such connatural objects in order to understand (as best we can) "matters divine" evoke the need for "spiritual exercises" on the part of philosophical inquirers? Here Hadot's focus on Plato can help us, along with the reflections his dialogues elicit about language. When Plato has Socrates give us his intellectual odyssey, in the *Phaedo,* detailing the move from "physical inquiry" to ethical questions, the turning point was Anaxagoras and his conviction that it is "intelligence that orders and is the reason for everything" (97c). The examples which he gives for the ordering power of intelligence, which quickly become Plato's "forms," are all couched in analogous terms, like 'beautiful' or 'good'. This means that we can only learn the proper use of such terms by invoking examples, and the examples we know how to present are those which correspond with our experience. Thus philosophers are urged to live in such a way as to acquire rich paradigms for beauty or goodness, much as we judge novelists by the accuracy with which their dramatization of character delineates the texture of human feeling. For Plato it is ever the person of Socrates, notably in the more dramatic dialogues, who exemplifies the paradigmatic meaning of key terms in the argument—like 'life' in the *Phaedo:* the life connatural to the principle of life, which cannot end, is best displayed in the manner in which Socrates guides that portentous discussion on the very cusp of his own death.

Otherwise such terms are merely *abstract,* as most students deem them to be. But to begin to follow Socrates' arguments— even the manifestly inadequate ones—in such a way as to ask what sort of efforts it may take on our part to appreciate the force of their key terms amounts to asking how we might live in such a way as to privilege those dimensions of our life which we normally do not. In that respect, the opening paean to "philosophers" and the way of life to which they are called does more than set the tone for the *Phaedo;* it reminds us what we will be asked to undertake in order to understand, to say nothing of assess, the arguments which Socrates will be presenting. I am suggesting that the reason we will be asked to undertake the requisite exercises lies with the very character of the language used to probe such dimensions of existence: we cannot grasp it in its proper semantic mode without realizing that it is inherently analogous. And analogous terms need to be anchored to a primary analogate, so that other uses can be related proportionally to that central use. Otherwise they will appear and be employed in a merely "abstract" manner, and prove unable to lead us on to an understanding beyond that connatural to us.[7] It is that "leading" function of language, dubbed *manuductio* ["taking by the hand and leading"] by Aquinas, which analogous terms exhibit so powerfully when they are properly used. But again, their proper use will require a mode of inquiry and of life which privileges certain paradigm instances over others: "spiritual exercises," if you will.

Another way to ask about the language peculiar to inquiries into the goals of human existence is to remind oneself that relating terms like 'good' or 'wise' to their paradigm cases demands a keen sense of judgment. That indeed is what analogous usage comes to in practice: locating the paradigm use which will govern the discourse in question, and learning how to relate other uses to that one. So, for example, a married couple of twenty-five years may well wonder whether they really understood what they were doing when they married, or even when they assessed their relationship at earlier intervals of their marriage. To place themselves back in time imaginatively would reveal that they certainly had no idea of the depths of the words they used at earlier times, yet they avowed them wholeheartedly nonetheless. From this later vantage point, which has become their new paradigm, they can see how earlier, as well as project how later, avowals might be understood analogously, with reference to the current paradigm case. What Hadot calls "spiritual exercises" are designed precisely to evoke in us new ways of seeing, fresh paradigm cases for orienting our use of multivalent terms like 'good' or 'wise'. And the ensuing efforts to relate our continuing usage to these new benchmarks will develop that discerning judgment required for proper analogous usage.

Discerning readers will detect in these descriptions an attempt to give some bite and substance to common talk about "experience," especially dear to inquiries in religious studies. Yet unless that talk be linked explicitly to linguistic use, it can fail to evoke any specific resonance in listeners. One of the signal achievements of the Oxford philosophy which Diogenes Allen imbibed has been to tie its assertions to the regularities (or vagaries) of language use, so invoking patterns discernible to all of us. Once that strategy is employed to characterize analogous usage, we are constrained, as we have seen, to identify requisite qualities other than language itself—like the judgment required to use it well. Those skills too can be detected in use, just as any body of worshippers learns to discriminate good preaching from bad, often by following the rule of thumb: do preachers pretend to comprehend what they are speaking about, or do they display that degree of "unknowing" that properly befits any discourse about things divine? Such judgments are part of any discourse associated with a trade, where know-how requires careful attention to our actions and to our speech.[8] So we return to the way in which philosophical theology depends crucially on practical reason, on "know-how," to conduct its inquiries. That is the intellectual skill which is developed by doing, by engaging in "spiritual exercises."

Plato set the stage for identifying these exercises descriptively by displaying for us a kind and quality of dialogue in which the doing of philosophy is itself a spiritual exercise. The point of the *Meno*, for example, can be exhibited by reflecting on the course of the dialogue itself, and by reminding oneself that however inadequate may be the definition of *virtue* which the interlocutors attain, the virtue in question has been abundantly exhibited in the no-holds-barred inquiry which knew that such a definition could not be its proper conclusion. Again and again, the sense of "unknowing" proper to philosophic discourse is displayed in the manner in which it is carried out. Dialogue or conversation itself becomes a key spiritual exercise, training us as we undertake the mode of inquiry proper to philosophy. In that sense, we are all always apprentices, just as teachers learn how to learn from their students in their effort to elicit from them the quality of response which assures that genuine teaching is taking place. That takes place, paradoxically enough, when teachers are not pretending to "teach" (in the accepted sense of that term) but are rather engaging others in an inquiry in which they themselves are already engaged, with no clear sense at all of its outcome. That is philosophical teaching at its best, as Plato displays so well in his dialogues and explicitly averts to in the *Meno*: a form of apprenticeship in which teacher and learner alike are being called forward by the *good* they are pursuing, and recognize in the course of their conversation that they are indeed being carried closer to their goal.

As some early Christian thinkers perceived, there turn out to be key similarities between dialogic encounter in response to the good and a set of spiritual exercises attuned to responding to the good news offered to human beings in Jesus. These affinities allowed Alexandrian thinkers like Clement and Origen to speak of Christian revelation as "revealed philosophy."[9] Yet the 'good' in "good news" is so much more specific, so much more able to be identified than Plato's *Good*, that response to it calls for a more deliberate and concentrated listening. In the risen Lord, the Lord of heaven and earth, the creator of all-that-is, is speaking to us individually and inviting each rational creature to a personal participation in the very life of God. That is an overwhelming prospect in Plato's own terms, so the listening component has to increase proportionally. Hence Christian prayer turns out to be more listening for the voice of the Lord than dialogic in character, though the speaker is also expressly an interlocutor: the Hebrew pattern of covenant and the cognate prayer pattern of *beraka* has informed Christian practice from the beginning. Since the initiative is so manifestly the Lord's, however, it behooves us to attend to what the Lord has to say, and try to tailor our response to the spontaneous and unearned gift of revelation. Such is the pattern of the Hebrew scriptures, canonized in Deuteronomy, which has shaped Christian prayer from the beginning.

Thus the "spiritual exercises" commended to Christians in their search for illumination from such a "revealed philosophy" focus on the eucharistic celebration: a prayer suffused with thanksgiving along the lines of the Hebrew *beraka*-formula: "Blessed are You, Lord God of the universe, who have. . . ."

We are initially reminded of a specific action of God on our be-half, and in recalling it we ask yet further blessings as a way of pledging our wholehearted response. Formation in such a mode of prayer is designed to work against our penchant to begin with our own capacities and desires and implore divine help to ful-fill *them*. Monastic *lectio divina* sits us down first to listen to the word of God, to savor it, and to hear it as addressed to us per-sonally. This has become the paradigmatic meditation form in Christianity, moving as it does from initially listening to scrip-ture to selecting verses which can act as mantras to focus our attention, so letting those words penetrate our heart. The step from many words to fewer and even to wordlessness becomes natural enough, yet the initiative remains with the Word of God. Such a "vertical" set of spiritual exercises, however, is com-plemented by conversation between persons formed in its pat-terns, conversation allowing them to seek to clarify together the truth revealed in the scriptures and appropriated by each of them personally.

The dual character of the basic Christian *Torah*, to love God and one's neighbor, demands that a "horizontal" set of exercises complement the "vertical" one, just as the norm for a whole-hearted monastic response to the Word became cenobitic or community-oriented. We have a poignant example of such a di-alogue in the ninth book of Augustine's *Confessions,* when he de-scribes his final encounter with his mother, Monica.

The conversation led us towards the conclusion that the plea-sure of the bodily senses, however delightful in the radiant light of this physical world, is seen by comparison with the life of eternity to be not even worth considering. Our minds were lifted up by an ardent affection towards eternal being itself. Step by step we climbed beyond all corporeal objects and the heaven itself. . . . We ascended even further by internal reflection and dialogue and wonder at your works, and we entered into our own minds. We moved up beyond them so as to attain to the region of inexhaustible abundance where you feed Israel eternally with truth for food. There life is the wisdom by which all creatures come into being. . . . (9.x [24])

It proves fascinating to compare this dialogic ascent with the account of his own ascent in book 7:

By the Platonic books I was admonished to return to myself [Plotinus, *Enneads* 4.1.1]. With you as my guide I entered into my innermost citadel . . . and with my soul's eye . . . saw above that same eye of my soul the immutable light higher than my mind. It was superior because it made me, and I was inferior because I was made by it. The person who knows the truth knows it and he who knows it knows eternity. Love knows it. Eternal truth and true love and beloved eternity: you are my God. (7.x [16])

Note how both accounts incorporate the distinctively Jewish and Christian identification of the Good with God as Lord of heaven and earth, creator of all-that-is, while relying on Platonic accounts of the mind's ascent to that One to give the contours of a rational creature's journey home.

In the dialogue of Augustine with his mother, the path of ascending is mutually confirming. At this point in their lives it becomes purely celebratory, of course, since his personal dialectical journey is over. Yet one does not have to imagine him in clarifying dialogue with other fellow-travelers; such conversations are recorded in explicit or implicit dialogue form in his subsequent writings. Even in his preaching, we find him dialoguing with his congregation, so ingrained is that form of communication in him. Yet even in the exercise of preaching, he dare not assume the role of master, for the master in such dialogues is "the immutable light higher than [our] minds," Christ himself. Conversation takes on a new cast, "for where two or three are gathered together in my name, I am there among them" (Mt 18:20). The personal presence of this light "through whom all things came into being" (Jn 1:3) hardly militates against vigorous dialectical exchange; in fact it encourages such exchange by confirming Socrates' conviction that persons engaged in pursuing the truth as they have come to know it can help one another to walk further along that path. Christ's presence confirms this conviction initially by revealing the contours of the path itself, and in practice by helping to free us interlocutors from our endemic tendency to defend our current stance, so that we can be open to others' correction. In this way, God's revelation to us in Jesus as the ordering wisdom through whom all things were made should enhance the classical spiritual exercise of dialogic search for truth, provided its new participants are concurrently steeped in the *lectio divina* which grants them the freedom of serving a master who is their very creator.

Friends then become friends in the one who offers us friendship with God (Jn 15:15), thus encouraging the kind and quality of exchange which Plato brings to life in the *dramatis persona* of Socrates. The rules of engagement with the master, Socrates, are not altered but intensified, as we are all called to a radical "unknowing" in the face of the offer of divine friendship extended to us, and thus are stimulated to let go of our endemic desire to protect our own life, reputation, and opinions. Friendship in Jesus does not rest on agreement so much as on an embracing good which is promised to each so long as they are willing to submit to the rule of learning from the Word of God and of testing their understanding of that word with one another. So friendship and inquiry coalesce in ways similar to those commended to us in the interaction of Socrates with his followers, and the interaction among friends becomes a prime example of a "spiritual exercise" in this community of inquiry which is that of "revealed philosophy."

## Notes

1. A selection of Diogenes Allen's writings should begin with *The Reasonableness of Faith* (Cleveland, Ohio: World Publishing, 1968), and continue with *Three Outsiders: Pascal, Kierkegaard, and Simone Weil* (Cambridge, Mass.: Cowley Publications, 1983), *Philosophy for Understanding Theology* (Atlanta: John Knox Press, 1985), and *Love: Christian Romance, Marriage, Friendship* (Cambridge, Mass.: Cowley Publications, 1987).

2. Pierre Hadot, *Philosophy as a Way of Life,* ed. Arnold Davidson (Cambridge, Mass.: Blackwell, 1995), 21, citing Hadot's "La philosophie antique: une éthique ou une pratique?" in *Problèmes de la morale antique,* ed. Paul Demont (Amiens, 1993), 11 (emphasis Davidson's).

3. Pierre Hadot, *Plotinus, or, The Simplicity of Vision,* trans. Michael Chase (Chicago: University of Chicago Press, 1993).

4. Hadot's extensive illustration of this point has recently been published in Paris by Gallimard: *Qu'est-ce que la philosophie antique?* (1995). Chapter 10 treats of Christianity defining itself as philoso-

phy, notably in Alexandria, and chapter 11 of the later medieval conception of philosophy as the handmaid of theology.

5. Aquinas' touted definition of a teacher, here extended to those who teach us by their texts. I have never been able to locate it in his works.

6. *Summa Theologiae* 1.84.7.

7. This view of analogous usage of language was first suggested to me by the early work of Ralph McInerny, work which has happily been recently reprised in his *Aquinas and Analogy* (Washington, D.C.: Catholic University of America Press, 1996).

8. This dimension of analogous usage is particularly well treated by James Ross in his *Portraying Analogy* (Cambridge: Cambridge University Press, 1981), esp. chap. 7: "Analogy and Religious Discourse: Craftbound Discourse."

9. Hadot, *Qu'est-ce que la philosophie antique?* chap. 10: "Christianity as Revealed Philosophy."

# 3

## The Role of Dialogue and Friendship in Cross-Cultural Understanding

Intercultural understanding may be compared to a continuous act of translating, yet translating knows no rules. In fact, the only rule one can follow is that of continual dialogue, for the effort of translating represents a constant challenge to try to understand the "other" in the other's own terms, so that we can render to our community what it is that has attracted us elsewhere. Yet nothing short of interpersonal exchange can sustain the attraction as well as challenge our penchant to misconstrue. I am presuming that the intercultural understanding which we seek responds to something more than curiosity in each of us, that we are attracted to something "other" out of an awakened feeling that the western Enlightenment view of the *humanum* does not and cannot tell the whole story. When this keen sense of needing another can be acted out in an enduring friendship, there is hope of mutual understanding. This feeling turned conviction becomes a useful shorthand for "postmodernism," where the "modern" can be linked with the hubris that *our* civilization offered humanity the paradigm for being human, so that colonialism could be presented as something nobler than mere exploitation, indeed, as the "white man's burden." The illustration is telling, however, for all of the characteristics of colonialism can be seen to derive from a *modern*, Enlightenment perspective, beginning with the impression that the newly "discovered" continents were virtually empty of people, however counterfactual that proved to be.

In my own fledgling discipline of comparative philosophical theology, it was Karl Rahner (in his seminal lecture delivered in Cambridge, Massachusetts, in 1979) who responded creatively to the feelings of young people, so evident during the 1960s, that Christianity was "missing something" that religious practices of the East could provide.[1] He contended that the real point of Vatican II, perceptible only in retrospect, proved to be its bringing to closure nineteen centuries of "western European Christianity," to present Christianity vis-à-vis other major religions of the world in a fashion quite different from anything in its history since the early "parting of the ways" to which Jewish believers in Jesus had to come to find a way to welcome pagans into the "new Israel." Rahner offered his retrospective reading of Vatican II as a "fundamental interpretation" of its contribution to the history of Christianity, "fundamental" in the sense of capturing a significance present yet hitherto unrecognized. He adduced as evidence movements away from Eurocentrism in political and cultural perceptions, thereby granting to this event a larger than ecclesial significance, as well as re-periodizing Christian history.

This reading of the council brought one of its lesser documents, *Nostra Aetate,* to the fore. Rahner noted that the major conciliar documents had all been preceded by decades of theological groundwork, while this one resulted from forces within the council itself and proceeded with little or no prior theological preparation. In fact, he cites it as reflecting and responding to a "theological crisis" in the life of the church, where decisions must be made without the benefit of developed categories. This fact especially signals the parallel with 70 A.D. and the vexing question whether pagan converts to Christianity had to be circumcised or not. Since the admission of gentiles into the "new Israel" signaled the beginning of the end of Jewish Christianity, 70 A.D. has long been used to mark the "parting of the ways" between Christianity and the Judaism given birth at Ramle. Surely part of Rahner's intent in offering this "fundamental" interpretation of the council, as well as so fresh a reading of Christian history, was to use the history of enmity between these two communities as a warning of what we must avoid in meeting yet other religious groups: if we can appreciate how new is the ground on which we are meeting them, Christians may be encouraged to present themselves in a posture fostering mutual acceptance and dialogue. What had become the standard interpretation of Vatican II—that the four-century standoff between Protestants and Catholics had been effectively mediated, at least, theologically—is here subsumed under a far wider view, enlarging the meaning of "ecumenism" and in effect relegating the Reformation to a blip on the screen.

In retrospect, we may hear Rahner's proposals as an early call to a "postmodern" view of matters wider in scope than the ecclesial ones to which he had addressed himself, yet which he had already seen as part of a larger movement. The Christianity of modernity, while shadowed by an Enlightenment account of human reason which found faith to be redundant to the *humanum* and even counted it a powerful obstacle to human aspirations, nonetheless enjoyed sufficient political support to retain a hegemonic position in the world. The missionary movement offers a prime example of this mentality. So the analysis of the internal relations of reason to power, delineated so effectively by Michel Foucault and others, can be extended to faith as well. Yet the new situation of Christianity vis-à-vis other major religions across the world feeds back on settled Christian regions to offer a fresh understanding of faith in relation to power and success. If we add to this attitude the attendant cultural movement described paradoxically as a "loss of faith in reason," we can see how prescient were Rahner's observations. Faith is no longer regarded as an "extra"; indeed, every inquiry is seen as beginning with presuppositions which have to remain unexamined at the outset. The critical question is no longer one of securing "indubitable foundations" but of assessing—retrospectively—the adequacy of one's presuppositions. In this sense, one may say that John Henry Newman won the nineteenth-century debate in the twentieth, probably more on the strength of historical events than on the persuasive power of reason—a fact he himself would surely have appreciated.

As a result of these interlocking movements we are being moved to consider all understanding as intercultural understanding and any act of reading as one of translating, and we are invited to view this situation as one of enrichment rather than estrangement. "No human being is an island" becomes "no culture can stand alone in defining or exemplifying the riches of human aspiration." Appreciating other cultures from study or travel becomes a call for multiculturalism at home. "Thick descriptions" of anthropology tend to overshadow survey methods in sociology, as researchers realize that even people inhabiting the same geographical space cannot be presumed to hear questions the same way. The fact that we can no longer presume a uniform cultural heritage in our students prompts some to bemoan the loss, yet moves others to exploit the differences palpably present. Whatever our reaction, however, this is the situation in which we currently live, dubbed "postmodern," even though that name only picks out its salient characteristics negatively and so includes many contenders. I shall contend that our current situation favors a reading of "objectivity" as "intersubjectivity," a proposal anticipated in midcentury by the Canadian philosophical theologian, Bernard Lonergan. It also explains the predilection for narrative over system, since stories become invaluable and inescapable modes of introduction when one can no longer presume a shared culture. Moreover, we may find that we did not share as much as the dominating culture presumed we all did, once we are pressed to articulate our own presuppositions in a framing story. Before offering a constructive account of this process, however, we need to "deconstruct" a specter, specifically that of *relativism.*

## 1. The Specter of Relativism

It is crucial to note how Enlightenment presuppositions about reason and truth gave that very specter its stature as a threat. For they presume a normative set of rational criteria available to all, against which any claim to other sets of criteria is utterly unsettling. That is what we mean by "relativism": there are no longer any operative norms across human discourse, so power or even violence will have to arbitrate. Yet like earlier debates over "natural law," there may be other ways of thinking about those criteria which are not laden with specific beliefs but which have to do with the fact that believers formed in quite diverse traditions can discourse with one another. Once the idol of "pure reason" has been shattered, and we can learn to accept diverse ways of arriving at conclusions, we will also find that we can employ the skills learned in our tradition to follow reasoning in another. Traditions, in other words, may indeed be *relative* to one another in ways that can prove mutually fruitful rather than isolating. Those traditions which prove to be so will be those which avail themselves of human reason in their development, and the patterns of stress and strain in their evolution will display their capacity for exploiting the resources of reason.[2] In short, "relativism" gives way to the human fact that all inquiry takes place within a tradition, and the specter which it evoked turns out to be the shadow of our faith in "pure reason," that is, in the possibility of human inquiry outside of any tradition.

The discovery (on the part of reason) that every inquiry employs presuppositions which cannot themselves be rationally justified opens the way to self-knowledge on the part of Enlightenment philosophy, which can then take its place among the traditions.[3] And once that has been accomplished, the specter of "relativism" dissolves in the face of developing the skills needed to negotiate among traditions, which can be negotiated because they can be seen to be related one to another. Since we have become accustomed to associating *faith* with *tradition,* we must then renounce the normative Enlightenment view which represented faith as an "addendum" to the human condition. If that view itself reflects a tradition whose account can be rendered in historical terms (as a reaction to the devastating religious wars in Europe), then it too will have a recognizable convictional basis, and faith will once more emerge as part of a shared human legacy. The intellectual task, on the part of reason operative in any tradition which survives the test of time, becomes one of learning how such traditions develop and how one might learn from the other. *Reason,* in other words, becomes a functional notion displayed in practices which cut across traditional boundaries, rather than a set of substantive beliefs which must be adhered to *in those very terms* before discourse can be undertaken. *Rationality* will show itself in practices which can be followed and understood by persons operating in similar fashion from different grounding convictions.[4]

What they have in common is the need to talk about what they believe. Here emerges the analogy with debates about "natural law": what is so shared and common as to be dubbed "natural" are not necessarily substantive norms regarding human actions so much as the demand that any normative "law" must express itself in a coherent discourse. That very activity, which displays the fruitfulness of human ingenuity, also contains operative parameters whose function can be tracked by astute participant-observers prepared to recognize analogies across traditions of inquiry. Socrates' assembling of linguistic reminders for Thrasymachus made him abandon his projected discourse, without Socrates having to exert any force at all (*Republic* bk. 1). For those reminders had to do with the possibility of any discourse at all, and thus governed the tradition Thrasymachus was defending as well as the totally opposed one which Socrates had set out to elaborate. Book 1 of the *Republic* does not defend Socrates' own position so much as it displays the terms for any debate. One may, of course, go on to imbed those terms in a much larger framework, as Plato does in the subsequent books of the *Republic,* but the exchange with Thrasymachus stands on its own as displaying the coherence of the very practice which makes the rest possible. We will need to elaborate that coherence into a "philosophy," for practice alone seldom offers a persuasive display of its own cogency. However, these reflections should remind us that the elaboration is secondary, and there may even be many such, though they will be able to be elucidated *relative* to one another. So the fact and the possibility of dialogue begins to emerge as the shape which reason takes in our pluralistic age.

Yet dialogue can only take place among persons; systems cannot converse with one another. And even dialogue between persons can degenerate into a "dialogue of the deaf" if each one comes as a "representative" of a position. The prerequisite for dialogue among persons seems to be a shared interest in pursuing the truth of the matter, no matter how deep and shaping are one's convictions on the subject. If those very convictions presume that the path one is traveling is the only way to arrive at truth in such matters, then the goal has already been circumscribed, and dialogue is rendered nugatory. We see that *truth* must transcend any given conceptuality, and that each participant must be committed to questing after it. Yet, as we have just remarked, what once seemed an obvious path is no longer available to us: namely, that philosophy, or untrammeled rational inquiry, represents a neutral achievement accessible to those willing to renounce their particular paths. In this sense, we cannot consistently espouse a "pluralism" which retains the modern presumption that we philosophers can survey diverse religious traditions from a superior vantage point.[5] The alternative to presuming such "objective" neutrality is to turn to an intersubjective encounter with persons prepared in the way we have described: willing to search together for the truth to which they are singly committed, yet which they may name quite differently. Such a commitment is uncannily close to a classical view of friendship first articulated by Aristotle.

## 2. Growth in Friendship and the Search for Truth

I would like to explore three ways in which developments in friendship parallel stages in the quest for understanding which sees itself as a search for truth. In fact, as I shall argue, the quest for understanding (which Aristotle identified as the paradigmatic human desire at the outset of his *Metaphysics*) can more easily be felt and regarded as constituting a search for truth when its internal links with friendship are revealed: felt to be so by inquirers themselves, and so regarded by those whose task it is to reflect on human knowing. I shall be guided by three mentors and friends in this exploration: Bernard Lonergan, Stanley Hauerwas, and Aurelius Augustine. It was Lonergan, in his masterwork, *Insight: A Study of Human Understanding,* who anticipated the critique of "foundationalism" in epistemology by starkly contrasting the "need for certitude" to the "quest for understanding," thus suggesting crucial metaphors and attitudes guiding our reflections on human knowing: its origins, its processes, and its outcomes.[6] A glance back at the *Discourse on Method* with that contrast in mind reveals the anxiety pervading Descartes' endeavor, allowing one to delineate a dimension of what became "Enlightenment rationality" which has often escaped philosophical commentary: the *need* for bedrock. We can see, with poignant hindsight, how the various proposals proffered to supply that need have failed to quench it, so it may prove more fruitful to expose the need itself, as Lonergan set himself to do.

## 2.1. Following Lonergan's Lead

Pursuing the path of exposing the need for certitude in modern epistemology makes it increasingly clear that all attempts to meet that need effectively render any *quest* redundant. For to be in possession of an unshakable *warrant* releases the tension of inquiry by assuring our grasp of the truth of the matter in question, allowing us to direct our energies to exploring its implications and so tidying up what Kierkegaard loved to caricature as "the system." By contrast, a quest must press onward, progressing at best asymptotically to its motivating goal. Historically, this telling opposition between *quest* and *need* can be observed by contrasting Plato's conflicting yet relentless attention to the *eros* of the inquiring mind with the onto-theological schemes of those Neoplatonisms which merged increasing semantic generality with metaphysical fruitfulness in a hierarchical advance towards the pinnacle of the One, from which all things emanate in an ordered fashion. To be sure, the most astute of them, Plotinus, took care to place that One beyond being and discourse, so that human knowledge could never attain to the metaphysical ground it could assert. Yet for all his insistence, the very scheme of "necessary emanation," modeled as it is on logical deduction, could not help but assimilate the One to "the First," and so jeopardize the "infinite qualitative difference" so central to the religious appeal of Plotinus' One.[7] For it was that "difference," secured by placing the One "beyond being," which assured that Plotinus' scheme could not be turned into a system, that the One would at best be the object of a continuing quest, and thus would offer the religious alternative to Christianity which Augustine perceived it to be.

Closer to home, the "Thomism" generated in Catholic philosophical circles in response to the impetus of Pope Leo XIII's encyclical *Aeterne Patris* tended ineluctably towards creating a Thomas Aquinas (always "St. Thomas" in those circles) who answered uniquely to that overpowering human need for certitude which Descartes had exposed and sought to satisfy. It was perhaps inevitable that Aquinas would take on such a *persona* in the pervasively Cartesian climate into which Leo XIII had sought to insert a powerful corrective. There were also institutional constraints which ironically accompanied a "mandated" philosophy: the army of teachers which had to be enlisted could hardly count on a plurality of genuine philosophical spirits.[8] Anyone acquainted with the instruction prevailing in that period could be forgiven the caricature of Thomism as that philosophy which set out to answer all of the questions one never had. Yet the historical studies inspired by that same movement revealed an Aquinas less preoccupied with system than with exploration, notwithstanding the fact that his presentation of any topic offers a veritable exemplar of order and clarity.[9]

Bernard Lonergan managed to convey that Aquinas to his students: one constantly searching for ways to put the philosophy which the West had so recently inherited at the service of Augustine's ideal of "faith seeking understanding." Signs of this exploring spirit lie in distinctions invariably made *ad hoc,* in the service of understanding, with little concern to correlate them with like-sounding distinctions made in other contexts. The Thomists' maxim, *Sanctus Thomas semper formaliter loquitur,* was belied by his texts. Aquinas was responding less to a need for certitude than to his own quest for understanding, fueled by a vibrant faith in a transcendent object of understanding rather than secured in an evidential ground for subsequent deductions. The sense in which theology could be *scientia* for him was a highly analogous and nuanced one, quite removed from the geometric ideal of Aristotle's *Posterior Analytics,* with which Aquinas was sufficiently familiar to observe that its operative paradigm best suits "the mathematical sciences."[10] For that theology, along with its philosophical complement of metaphysics, tends towards an object who will not be anything other than subject, whose very essence is simply to exist. No "onto-theology" for Aquinas, since the spirit guiding his transformation of the philosophy which he found so useful was the distinction of creator from creation—a *distinction* utterly unlike any of those which philosophers find so useful in their attempts to find the "true joints" of the world. For it cannot be found *in* the world which lies exposed to human reason, but is only "glimpsed on the margin of reason," or "at the intersection of faith and reason," announcing as it does the inexpressible relation of free creator to creation.[11]

While that relation of creator to creatures may not be expressible, it can be lived out in those communities—Jewish, Christian, or Muslim—which have become repositories of the revelation of a free creation.[12] This elusive "distinction" will be able to be lived out in these communities to the extent that they offer the kind of mutual support which alone can allow us human beings to escape the imperious demands of our need for certitude. Indeed, the more one reflects on what Kierkegaard loved to call "Socratic unknowing," the more one realizes how ideal a type Plato's Socrates must be. For nothing seems more difficult for us as human beings than to continue the quest, making one more "fresh start," without the support of the bedrock we yearn for. Here, ironically enough, is where we find faith and a faith-community able to sustain us in actually living up to Socrates' ideal. It is ironic for us, at least, because those "masters of suspicion," Marx and Freud, long ago persuaded the intellectual world of the completeness of Enlightenment rationality by caricaturing faith as a "failure of nerve," and faith-communities as refuges for those so impaired. That caricature can persist even after the pretensions of Enlightenment rationality to completeness have been exposed. So it is best to return to our paradigm of friendship for faith, which accounts for the persistence of such communities as well as hedges them against ideology.

Jesus invites his listeners to follow him if they are to understand what he is saying, and enjoins his followers, on the threshold of his passion and death, no longer to think of themselves as his servants but as his friends (Jn 15:15). The first letter of John reminds us that we can only be his friends as we learn how to befriend one another (1 Jn 4:21).[13] The sense that this expression has in both places amounts to accompanying another on the journey of faith in the God who bridges what Aristotle deemed to be an unbridgeable divide in offering us divine friendship in Jesus.[14] We each have some experience of what that accompaniment amounts to: it is never mindless or uncritical "support," which presumes that one's friends are beyond correction, worthy of nothing but adulation and confirmation in their manner of life. It rather consists in mutually recalling a shared commitment, as well as subtle counsel regarding appropriate role models within the rich panoply of potential guides in the larger community. In this way our current friends open us to friends of theirs, living or dead, and the cross-hatching of such friendships transforms what we call community and tradition into accessible resources. That is, friends give life to those terms by making community and tradition present to us as realities sustaining us.

This "actuation" is particularly vivid when the realities in question are animated by divine revelation, itself a renewal of the present-making activity of creation. For such a revelation is only carried by doctrine in a secondary mode: doctrine, as George Lindbeck has forcibly reminded us, represents the grammar of practices, practices into which neophytes are initiated and which evolve in relation to the cultural realities of successive times.[15] Our relation to our mentors, to those whom we admire for their adeptness at such practices, comes to constitute what we call community and tradition. The master/disciple model for education in all religious traditions provides the key to this process: learning is not ingesting "material" but assimilating practices, developing specific virtues which will allow disciples, as they become proficient, to outstrip their masters. That both master and disciple are apprenticed to a tradition of revelatory texts reinforces rather than stifles students' creativity, for the structure of their interaction constantly reminds masters that they are, at best, "inadequate, secondary causes," as Aquinas is said to have characterized the teacher. Something of that sort must have animated the sixteenth-century return to scripture, although from our perspective the attempt to divorce revelatory texts from their history of interpretation was bound to prove one-sided. For texts require communities, as community requires a texture of friendships.

## 2.2. Stanley Hauerwas's Theological Friendship

We have already heard Stanley Hauerwas insisting that friendship consists "in our willingness to place our life and needs in the hands of another."[16] This is part of a sustained rereading of Aristotle on friendship, helped along by the revelation of God in Christ refracted through Aquinas—something neither Aristotle nor any other human being could ever have imagined. While Aristotle's account of friendship in the concluding books of the *Nicomachean Ethics* supplants his ideal of the "magnanimous man" arising from his account of virtue in the early books of that work, he has difficulty to the end in seeing how we could ask friends to share in our bad fortune, for that would bring them pain (9.11). Vulnerability remains a problem to the extent that the "magnanimous man" continues to hover over the work. As Hauerwas puts it: "our friendship with God does rest on his vulnerability as we believe God has and continues to take the risk that his kingdom depends on the faithfulness of our response" (13). This observation reminds one of Etty Hillesum's prescient response (*avant la lettre*) to Elie Wiesel's complaints (in *Night*) about God's absence from Auschwitz: "One thing is becoming increasingly clear to me: that You cannot help us, that we must help You to help ourselves. And that is all we can manage these days and also all that really matters: that we safeguard that little piece of You, God, in ourselves. And perhaps in others as well. . . . You cannot help us but we must help You and defend Your dwelling place inside us to the last."[17]

To accept the other as our friend not only involves "extending to one's friend the same relation one has to oneself" (*Nicomachean Ethics* 9.4, 1166a30); it means that in accepting another to be my friend I open that relating which is myself to interaction with another, making myself vulnerable to them as they become so to me. Aristotle hinted at this process of mutual becoming at the very end of his treatment when he noted how "the friendship of the good . . . increases in goodness because of their association" (9.12, 1172a12). But just as the ideal of the "magnanimous man" was associated with a self-sufficient view of self-as-substance, the subsequent recognition that "a good friend is by nature desirable for a good man" (9.9, 1170a14) would require a view of self-as-relating only dimly perceived by Aristotle through the prism of friendship. A consistent elaboration of this view of the human person would have to wait for Søren Kierkegaard's treatment (as Anti-Climacus) in *Sickness unto Death,* where he contrasted his proposal to regard the self-as-relation, indeed, "the relation's relating to itself," with the accustomed definition (from Aristotle through Hegel) of the self as "a synthesis . . . , a relation between two terms."[18] Be those terms Aristotle's 'rational' and 'animal', or Hegel's 'finite' and 'infinite', 'temporal' and 'eternal', 'freedom' and 'necessity', the person remained defined by categories accessible to philosophy, whereas Kierkegaard's proposal derived from the Cappadocians' exploitation of the single category of Aristotle which ill fit his metaphysics of substance, namely, relation, in order to articulate the difference in persons within the one God of Israel newly revealed in Jesus. The "Father, Son, and Spirit" of scripture could be expressed as "subsistent relations" without offending the principle of God's simpleness and oneness, precisely because *relation* proved to be so elusive a category in Hellenistic metaphysics. By appropriating that same category to explicate self as *spirit*, Kierkegaard succeeded in a single stroke to indicate the uniqueness of human beings in creation, as well as their "likeness to God."

All that is by way of reminding us that while Aristotle seemed to get the "facts" of friendship quite right, he still lacked the conceptuality to explicate properly what he had observed and experienced. That had to wait for a theological assist. Similarly, his observation that friends "desire to spend their lives with their friends" (9.12, 1172a6) adumbrates the way in which, Hauerwas insists, "friendships require as well as acquire a history . . . that provides a common memory and life" (12). Here again, revelation reinforces experience, as we realize in consciously shaping our lives to the models of scripture: while friendship with God is made possible by that mysterious elevation of mind and heart called "grace," it takes shape only through the history fashioned by our relating with God and others who also share this friendship with God. The experience over time of fidelity shows us that friendship is far more than a "metaphor for understanding our relation with God; it is in effect a crucial exercise for learning what it means to have our lives bounded by God's love" (Hauerwas, 14). As the way to understanding involves "learning how" more than "learning that," so becoming friends with those who have also allowed themselves to become friends with God entails the exercises appropriate to such a life, and will result in the understanding of community and of tradition that we have attempted to sketch above. Again, the experience and the divinely issued invitation illuminate one another, emboldening us to enter into that otherness within as we allow ourselves to encounter others who have themselves allowed the Other in— as Etty Hillesum aptly put it.

This shared experience of becoming friends of God, in Christ, teaches us other things as well. It is the crucible within which we learn how properly to "name" God; that is, how to use those terms which we must use to call attention to God, yet which in their ordinary uses can only mislead us. The tradition calls this analogous language, yet no satisfactory account of such usage seems to have been forthcoming. The exercise of friendship tells us why: there is none, so none should be expected.[19] There can be no *theory* of analogy precisely because the expressions which we call "analogous" are those which we need to use in situations so diverse that the appropriateness cannot be mapped. This is clearly the case in bridging the "ontological difference" separating creatures from creator, but it can be illustrated in privileged human situations as well. The couple who insist on their twenty-fifth anniversary that they did not know what 'love' meant when they exchanged it on their first anniversary are certainly speaking the truth in giving voice to the experiential gap between these two dates. Yet they also spoke truly on that first anniversary in saying they loved one another. Terms like 'love' are inherently context-dependent, in such a way that our primary or orienting sense is constantly shifting. The fact that it can continue to shift testifies to the transcendent dimension of such terms. Without that testimony we would have nothing but conventional morality; Socrates' celebrated paradox about wisdom indicates that we will never grasp the full meaning of such terms, so they are apt for use *in divinis*.

How, then, can we get our bearings? By continuing the journey of understanding to which such terms invite us, revising at each discernible stage the narrative which impels us, and so taking our bearings from past experience. Here is where the autocritical dimensions of tradition become operative, in the attempts of its adherents to take their own bearings in relation to the originating revelational texts as they let those texts shape their lives. For their lives will also be imbedded in cultures in part antithetical to the revelation which they adopt as their guide, so they will be called upon to craft anew their story as they try to live it out. Thus the operative terms will be tested as to how well they continue to call us forth and to illuminate our way in the world in which we live. This process, which I have called "retrospective verification," effectively translates Newman's thesis in his *Grammar of Assent,* as conveyed in Nicholas Lash's introduction to a recent edition.[20] It should be clear by now that we could never undertake this process alone; the flexibility which self-criticism demands calls for the candid assessment which only friends can provide, friends who share in the project of friendship with Christ primarily, but also others who are seeking to return all they have received to the One who has freely bestowed it. So long as we are intent upon such a journey, we will appreciate the need for analogous expressions to convey the continuity and the newness of the journey, and also find that we become used to employing these terms in fresh ways in new contexts without losing touch with their import. In fact, nothing can be more exasperating on such a journey than the demand on the part of someone on the sidelines for an unequivocal—that is, univocal—description of what it is we are about.

## 2.3. Augustine: Friends Alone Can Show the Way

What we are seeking for here is what one might call an "embodied understanding."[21] Augustine's *Confessions* was intended to offer us just that, as he mined his memory to discover for himself and also to show us the ways in which God had led him to the point where he could begin to return all that he had so freely been given. Much has and should be made of book 7, where he discovers how to negotiate the two outstanding questions which stood between him and an assent of faith: how properly to conceive of God, and how to think about evil. The celebrated ladder of ascent in 7.17 gave him an idiom for speaking of God as the "light of the light of my soul." That allowed him to see "that all finite things are in you, not as though you were a place that contained them, but . . . they are in you because you hold all things in your truth as though they were in your hand" (7.15). Discovering the order in his own reasoning powers, as he ascended "from the consideration of material things to the soul, . . . and then to the soul's inner power . . . beyond which dumb animals cannot go, [and thence to] the power of reason, [and finally to] judgment" (7.17), he was able to experience a nonspatial realm and so gain access to a language for "the God who IS" (7.17).

Yet this is far from the end of the road. In fact, Augustine is dismayed at this point to find that "I had no strength to fix my gaze on the [One who IS, but] recoiled and fell back into my old ways" (7.17), so "I began to search for a means of gaining the strength I needed to enjoy you" (7.18). This, he avers, "I could not find . . . until I embraced the *mediator between God and men, Jesus Christ, who is a man, like them* [1 Tim 2:5] yet also *rules as God over all things, blessed forever* [Rom 9:5]. He was calling to me and saying *I am the way; I am truth and life* [Jn 14:6]" (7.18). For as yet, he realized, "I was not humble enough to conceive of the humble Jesus Christ as my God, nor had I learnt what lesson his human weakness was meant to teach" (7.18). This will come as he reaches out to others, and becomes willing to place his life in their hands to the extent that he lets himself be guided by their witness. This is one more place where we can note how the *Confessions* is pointedly crafted to show us the way beyond "the Platonists" to whom Augustine has just acknowledged his indebtedness.[22] At the end of book 7, he already sees how he had to move beyond them: "none of this [about Jesus] is contained in the Platonists' books. Their pages have not the mien of the true love of God. . . . It is one thing to descry the land of peace from a wooded hilltop; . . . it is another to follow the high road to that land of peace, the way that is defended by the care of the heavenly Commander" (7.21). That journey will be motivated and undertaken on the strength of others' witness.

Book 8 begins with reference to his "heart," which seemed to be the proper focus of attention once the intellectual obstacles had fallen away.[23] Whereupon he notes: "By your inspiration it seemed to me a good plan to go and see Simplicianus who, as I could see for myself, was a good servant of yours" (8.1). And Simplicianus tells him "about Victorinus, whom he had known intimately when he was in Rome" (8.2). So we have a tableau of imbedded witnesses, to whom Augustine looks for the courage to take the step which he knows is the right one for him. All this seems quite opposed to the inner journey of intellectual warrant which had given him a language for speaking of God as a nonmaterial being. That rendition laid bare his capacities for understanding and judgment, and while these led him beyond themselves to their source, it was nonetheless an intellect aware of its own capacities which evoked that experience and that idiom. Here is a person all too aware that he lacks the strength to act on what he has seen, who seeks out the witness of fellow-travelers. Not that *their* actions can simply be made his; he spontaneously seeks God's help in the wake of his encounter: "Come, O Lord, and stir our hearts. Call us back to yourself" (8.4). Then begins the celebrated reflection on will: "When your servant Simplicianus told me the story of Victorinus, I began to glow with fervour to imitate him . . . , but I was held fast . . . by my own will, which had the strength of iron chains" (8.5). And that dilemma will not be resolved until the moment in the garden, when he returns to the language of "heart," noting how, "in an instant, as I came to the end of the sentence, it was as though the light of confidence flooded into my heart and all darkness of doubt was dispelled" (8.12).

We have focused on the crucial passage of the *Confessions,* a passage from mind to heart, which is recorded as a personal transformation intimately connected to Augustine's relations with others who shared the faith to which he felt called but unable to embrace. There is no opposition between others and self here, when those others are already living in the relationship with God which he desires for himself. It is as if that relationship of friendship with God in Christ, which will bind the pilgrims together as friends, is one into which others are invited to enter. We can only learn how to be friends with God from those who have learned already, and it turns out that they have learned from others as well. That is the cross-hatching of friendships which makes for community. The finale of Augustine's story invites us to reread it with an eye for friendship, noting how the pear-tree incident teaches him that buddies are not always friends (2.6–10), as well as how a friend's embrace of the faith and subsequent death brought Augustine up short in the life-project in which he was then engaged: "My heart grew sombre with grief, and wherever I looked I saw only death" (4.4–8). This event and its aftermath evoked an explicit reflection on friendship and its poignancy without a sustaining envelope of faith, by contrast with "those who love you, O God, and love their friends in you" (4.9).

The quest for understanding some things may be able to be carried out alone. But for those things too close to us to be able to discern, like our own heart, or so intimately sustaining of us that we cannot gain an independent purchase on them, like God properly conceived, we find that we need the context of a community of friendships to get our own bearings. As paradoxical as this sounds, since such things are apparently more intimately connected with our very selves than more "objective" situations, Augustine felt he had made a signal advance when he came to appreciate how much he "believed on the word of friends or doctors or various other people. Unless we took these things on trust, we should accomplish absolutely nothing in this life" (6.5). Here he deftly distinguishes the role of friends, who will help him become accustomed to this affront to his erstwhile autonomy as well as teach him how to go on in this newfound grasp of the ways of human understanding, from a conviction which he finds will not leave him: "in all the books of philosophy which I had read no misleading proposition, however contentious, had been able, even for one moment, to wrest from me my belief in your existence and in your right to govern human affairs; and this despite the fact that I had no knowledge of what you are" (6.5). This observation is particularly valuable for appreciating how a quest for understanding contrasts with the need for certitude. He continues: "My belief that you existed and that our well-being was in your hands was sometimes strong, sometimes weak, but I always held to it even though I knew neither what I ought to think about your substance nor which way would lead me to you or lead me back to you" (6.5).

Here we have three levels carefully distinguished: a sustaining faith ("my belief that you existed and our well-being was in your hands"), a current set of conceptual tools ("[how] I ought to think about"), and a whole-hearted response ("lead *me* to you"). He identifies the first as a mysteriously unyielding fact about himself and his own personal mindset, he is constantly seeking others' help to correct the second, though he undertakes it as his own personal responsibility, while the last (we have seen) inherently requires the assistance of others: their witness and their encouragement—"a friend is as another self" (Aristotle). So a full-blooded understanding, one which engages the entire person in a discriminating and discerning assent to what one has come to regard as true, can never be a solitary endeavor. We are too much in our own way, and are especially led astray by the multiple desires of our wayward hearts. This observation should remind us that, far from being the first autobiography, Augustine's *Confessions* represents anti-autobiography, seeking not for an elusive *self* but for its transcendent source, which is nonetheless closer to us than our very selves. And it is more dependable, as being the very truth of ourselves, the "light of the light of our souls." If that sounds like will-o-the-wisp language, the invitation of the *Confessions* is to entrust our own search for our self to Augustine's tutelage. If we can place that search in his hands, he will attempt to teach us how to displace it altogether, showing how one of our potential friends—himself—let it be transformed into a search for the source of all, including that precious self. Then we will be empowered to spend it in the service of others, as a part of our project of returning it to the One who gives it so freely and abundantly.

## 3. From "Objectivity" to "Intersubjectivity"

What may have appeared to be an *excursus* on friendship turns out to show us that a commitment to truth may be barely intelligible in other than personal terms. And attempting to understand the shaping convictions of other persons becomes the best access we can have to a view of truth as personal. It will take a tradition shaped by revelation to give proper voice to truth as personal, where God *speaks* in a language accessible to us. Significantly enough, those traditions which are so shaped invariably speak of a *path* and a *journey* of faith. God's word presents a challenge to understanding rather than a certitude made easily available. Our location in a world where diverse traditions become aware of their mutual presence to one another invites us precisely "on a voyage of discovery stripped of colonizing pretensions: an invitation to explore the *other* on the way to discovering ourselves."[24] I have suggested that the optimum way of responding to this invitation, so eloquently framed by the French Islamicist Roger Arnaldez, is by cultivating friends among those "others," who can then become companions along the way, without ceasing to be *other*. The precise manner in which explicitly diverse paths become a way defies logic, much as translating knows no firm rules. Yet the challenge to render another's convictions intelligible to oneself without making them over into one's own embodies the act of translating, which requires subtle judgments of similarity-cum-difference, thus exploiting to the full those analogous expressions which structure properly religious discourse.[25]

Philosophers habitually tend to shy away from analogous discourse, preferring the *terra firma* of univocity. Yet the quality of exchange among friends, which can allow for a common pursuit along different paths, requires the capacity inherent in analogous terms to let similarities retain their differences. Otherwise, communication will always presuppose agreement, requiring us to frame our convictions in a common language before we can be said to share them. What is peculiar about faith convictions, however, is precisely the way in which attempting to understand other paths can enrich our journey along our own. From this fact, like the practice of translating, we can counter the philosopher's penchant for univocal speech with an experience which requires another kind of language and reminds us how frequently we have recourse to it in conversations which engage our own convictions with others who may differ, even radically. Since it is unlikely that we should engage in such conversations in an unthreatening way except with friends, I have focused on friendship as a prerequisite for the quality of intersubjectivity which can come to substitute for *objectivity* in a postmodern context. Yet even more internally, as we have seen, the journey shared with friends becomes a paradigm of that quest for truth which displays to us the ubiquity and necessity of analogous discourse in negotiating the way set out before us.

## Notes

1. Karl Rahner, S.J., "Towards a Fundamental Interpretation of Vatican II," *Theological Studies* 40 (1979): 716–27.

2. Alasdair MacIntyre, *Whose Justice? Which Rationality?* chaps. 18–19.

3. Ibid., chap. 17.

4. Here, the reference is usually to the work of Ludwig Wittgenstein, notably the *Philosophical Investigations* (New York: Macmillan, 1956), and the extensive elaboration of reason as a human practice, which that seminal work spawned.

5. This would be my critique of John Hick's *particular* presentation of "pluralism": "Religious Particularity and Truth," in *Hermeneutics, Religious Pluralism, and Truth,* ed. Gregory D. Pritchard (Winston-Salem, N.C.: Wake Forest University, 1989), 35–49, followed by an exchange with John Hick and Ninian Smart.

6. *Insight: A Study in Human Understanding* (New York: Philosophical Library, 1957); 5th edition revised and augmented by Fred-

erick E. Crowe and Robert M. Doran, as vol. 3 in *Collected Works of Bernard Lonergan* (Toronto: University of Toronto Press, 1992).

7. See Lloyd Gerson, *God and Greek Philosophy* (New York: Routledge, 1990), chapter on Plotinus; Richard Walzer, *Al-Farabi on the Perfect State* (New York: Clarendon Press, 1985); David Burrell, *Knowing the Unknowable God* (Notre Dame, Ind.: University of Notre Dame Press, 1986).

8. I owe this astute observation to the late Ignatius Bochenski, who used to remark that the shortcomings of Thomism were inevitable and sociological, rather than philosophical: to demand so many teachers of any philosophy would assure that most of them would be less than qualified!

9. I am thinking especially of seminal works like M.-D. Chenu, *La Théologie au douzième siècle* (Paris: Vrin, 1957).

10. *In Posteriorum Analyticorum,* Liber 1, lectio 1 [10] (Milano: Marietti, 1955). See also M.-D. Chenu, *La Théologie comme science au treizième siècle* (Paris: Vrin, 1958), which comments sensitively on the way in which Aquinas transforms the Aristotelian ideal of *scientia* in his *Summa Theologiae,* notably 1.1.

11. See Robert Sokolowski, *The God of Faith and Reason* (Notre Dame, Ind.: University of Notre Dame Press, 1982), 39; also Josef Pieper, *The Silence of St. Thomas* (New York: Pantheon, 1957), and David Burrell, *Freedom and Creation in Three Traditions* (Notre Dame, Ind.: University of Notre Dame Press, 1993).

12. This is Sokolowski's astute observation, though he is more insistent than I that this is a "Christian" revelation. While I acknowledge his arguments that it is best displayed there, particularly in the controversies surrounding the ontological constitution of Jesus, culminating in Chalcedon, I am also struck by the fact that Christians share with Jews and with Muslims (as *Nostra Aetate* underlines) this revelation of God as the free creator of the universe, and that we are only beginning to see the implications of this shared (preposterous)

belief. See *God of Faith and Reason,* chap. 4: "The Incarnation and the Christian Distinction."

13. The operative words in 1 John are ever forms of *agapé,* and not of *philia,* which appears in John 15, yet the sense of transforming ordinary relationships and self-perceptions remains the same.

14. Aristotle, *Nichomachean Ethics* bk. 9.

15. *The Nature of Doctrine* (Philadelphia: Westminster, 1984).

16. Manuscript entitled "Friendship: An Exercise in Theological Understanding," delivered at a colloquium in the Department of Theology, University of Notre Dame, 9 May 1980.

17. Etty Hillesum, *An Interrupted Life* (New York: Washington Square Press, 1985), 186–87.

18. *Sickness unto Death*, trans. Alasdair Hannay (New York: Penguin, 1989), 43.

19. Nicholas Lash offers a persuasive view of this situation in his "Ideology, Metaphor and Analogy," in *Philosophical Frontiers of Christian Theology,* ed. Brian Hebblethwaite and Stewart Sutherland (Cambridge: Cambridge University Press, 1982), 68–94.

20. See my "Religious Belief and Rationality," in *Rationality and Religious Belief,* ed. C. F. Delaney (Notre Dame, Ind.: University of Notre Dame Press, 1979), and Newman, *An Essay in Aid of a Grammar of Assent.*

21. I have argued that this is precisely the kind of "foundation" which Lonergan calls for, which quite removes him from any "foundationalist" position: "Method and Sensibility: Novak's Debt to Lonergan," in *Journal of the American Academy of Religion* 40 (1972): 349–67.

22. For the way in which Augustine structures the *Confessions* to carry us with him beyond Neoplatonism, see John Cavadini, "Time and Ascent in *Confessions* XI," in *Collectanea Augustiniana 2: Presbyter Factus Sum,* ed. J. Lienhard, E. Muller, and R. Teske (New York: Peter Lang, 1993), 171–85.

23. I have presented a reading of the *Confessions* in which the odd-numbered chapters offer an intellectual articulation of a particular issue, which will only be fully resolved in the subsequent even-numbered chapter, where the steps will have to be taken to realize in a person's life what they have come to understand: *Exercises in Religious Understanding* (Notre Dame, Ind.: University of Notre Dame Press, 1973), chap. 1: "Augustine: Understanding as a Personal Quest."

24. Roger Arnaldez, *Three Messengers for One God,* trans. Gerald Schlabach (Notre Dame, Ind.: University of Notre Dame Press, 1994), vii. [Original edition: *Trois messagers pour un seul Dieu* (Paris: Albin Michel, 1983).]

25. On the role of judgment in using analogous expression properly, see my *Analogy and Philosophical Language* (New Haven: Yale University Press, 1973). For an application to central questions of philosophical theology, see the essay by Nicholas Lash (note 19) and my "Aquinas and Scotus: Contrary Patterns for Philosophical Theology," in *Theology and Dialogue: Essays in Conversation with George Lindbeck,* ed. Bruce Marshall (Notre Dame, Ind.: University of Notre Dame Press, 1990), 105–29.

# 4

# Friendship with God in al-Ghazali and Aquinas

Late-twentieth-century demagogues have exploited centuries of mutual disdain between Islam and Christianity to incite intergroup hatred and to unleash horrors against the weaker group. Yet the contrary fact remains: the groups that were incited to "ethnic cleansing" had also lived together for centuries, trading feasts and intermarrying. Similarly, during an earlier belligerent period, that of the crusades, some elements on both sides found themselves engaged in a quest for understanding which found thinkers of the three traditions of "the book" moving on parallel and often intersecting trajectories. Having explored the more metaphysical issues connected with the relations between the universe and its creator, and more recently between free creatures and the free creator of all, I should like here to essay some reflections on a theme closer to our subject of friendship.[1] Specifically, the theme is friendship with God, something deemed impossible by Aristotle, and certainly considered unseemly for Muslims, given the stereotype which has accumulated during the centuries of disdain. Yet I shall try to show how friendship with God is not only rendered possible by the revelation of a free creator in the Bible and Qur'an, it also delineates a paradigmatic way of free creatures relating to that creator in both Islam and Christianity. And no wonder, since the spiritual ancestor of both, Abraham, the one whom "God chose for friend" (Qur'an 4:125), "was called 'the friend of God'" (Jas 2:23).[2]

## 1. Some Common Factors

It is notoriously difficult to speak for traditions so variegated as Christianity and Islam, yet it will suffice to show that a thinker given central place in each not only finds room for friendship with God but indeed makes that theme the axial point of his exposition of the relationship between the creator and free creatures. Such an exploration will also allow me to commend the writings of two colleagues and friends, Paul Wadell and Marie-Louise Siauve. Wadell's recent *Friends of God: Virtues and Gifts in Aquinas* is a masterful condensation of a ten-year inquiry, and Marie-Louise Siauve's *L'amour de Dieu chez Gazâlî* presents an integrative study of that thinker which complements her translation of his book devoted to "love (*mahabba*), ardent desire (*shawq*), intimacy (*uns*), and perfect contentment (*ridâ*)" in his magnum opus, *Ihyâ' 'Ulûm ad-Dîn.*[3] I translated the book preceding this one in the *Ihyâ',* and in doing so discovered how Mlle. Siauve's study of the role which love plays in Ghazali's presentation of the relation of creatures to creator helps us reassess the philosophical acumen of that religious thinker. And while Aquinas' role as a philosopher is not in question, the angle of vision and appreciation to which Wadell introduces us remind

us how decidedly theological was Aquinas' appropriation of
Aristotle. Moreover, there is little evidence of "influence" of Ghazali on Aquinas, who was apparently acquainted only with
Ghazali's extended introduction to his celebrated attack on "philosophy" as he knew it (the *Tahâfût al-Falâsifâ*). Published separately as the *Maqâsid al-Falâsifâ*, this work presented the positions of the Islamic *falâsifâ* so fair-mindedly that western readers
like Aquinas mistook Ghazali for one of them.[4]

We have here a fascinatingly parallel treatment of friendship
with God by two religious thinkers, each concerned to present
his respective tradition in a way that underscored its capacity
to serve as a more comprehensive vehicle of the creator-creature
relationship than the current philosophical syntheses could de-
liver. Indeed, the perspective was not a merely speculative one
for either of them; Aquinas' treatment is imbedded in the first
part of the second part of the *Summa Theologiae*, which delineates
the manner of creatures' return to their source and origin in the
God who freely creates them, while the entire structure of Ghazali's *Ihyâ'* reflects his conviction that faithful practice alone confirms and explicates the meaning of what one might manage to
state in a more conceptual idiom.

While there is no evidence that Ghazali was directly be-
holden to Aristotle, as Aquinas was, the philosophic climate in
which his thought moved was redolent of both Aristotle and
Plato. So it would be best to begin, in any case, with some reminders from books 8–9 of the *Nicomachean Ethics*. This is particularly useful for moderns, whose notions of friendship tend
to be romantic in character, and who imagine relations to ter-
minate directly in the individuals concerned, as the simplest
parsing of "John loves Mary." Yet for Aristotle, friendship is en-
demically triadic: if John indeed loves Mary, then they must each

be oriented to an overarching (and interpenetrating) *good*, in which they can both share. That orientation to the *good* in each of them is what constitutes their proper character, so that Aristotle can insist not only that "friendship is a kind of partnership," but that one "stands in the same relation to his friend as to himself" (1171b33). This image of the individual as one who is "in relationship" suggests that a recasting of Aristotle's *Ethics* in the light of both of these books would yield an ideal quite different from "the magnanimous man." For that one was deemed to be "self-sufficient [and hence in] no need of friends" (1169b5), but when we adjust our optic to "happiness as a kind of activity" (1169b32) rather than something which can be attributed to a person, we are prepared to see ourselves as inherently relating beings, and the culmination of this turn of argument sees "a friend [as] by nature desirable for a good man" (1170a12). "By nature," we know, is Aristotle's most telling argument; in this case it also seems to be the one which he invokes not quite knowing how to emend his earlier substance-anthropology, in which individuals acquired virtues.

Aristotle's remarks in this context on self-love recall the Platonic divisions within the self—"the good man in relation to himself . . . is completely integrated and desires the same things with every part of his soul" (1166a12)—so there is already at work an inwardly relational view of human subjects. Something similar was invoked at the end of book 5, where Aristotle asks whether one can treat oneself unjustly or not (once justice has been construed as a societal virtue): "in a metaphorical and analogical sense there is such a thing as justice not towards oneself but between certain parts of the self [wherein] the rational is contrasted with the irrational part of the soul" (1138b5).

What the Bible and Qur'an add to this discussion, however, is the possibility—indeed the requirement—of intentional creatures relating to the source of their very being, their creator. Once God is revealed to be the originating source of all that is, and intentional creatures are invited to respond to the One as the source of their existence, the meaning of *divinity* is substantially altered from Aristotle's use of the term. So while the inequality-factor (which made friendship between humans and gods impossible for Aristotle [1158b30]) is pushed to infinity, the question of the possibility of friendship is posed anew by the fresh terms used to name the *relata:* creator and creature. Hence Aquinas will state that the very to-be of creatures is to-be-related to the One from which their existence derives: created to-be *is* a relation to its uncreated source, to-be itself (cf. *ST* 1.44–45).

While Ghazali does not articulate his metaphysics in so lapidary a fashion, he takes his stand on the implications of Islamic *tawhîd* (faith in divine unity): "there is no activity outside of God, who has brought forth and created all that is . . . without assistance of any sort."[5] Islamicists will detect echoes of al-Ash'arî in the precise use of 'activity' here; we may treat as moot that complex question for the moment, in the interest of comparing these two thinkers and of focusing on their shared legacy from the doctrine of free creation of the universe: human beings, created in the image of the creator, are called upon to live a wholehearted response to the gift of life which they are. For the doctrine of free creation entails that our life *is* gift, not *a* gift which we were somehow around to receive; it is we ourselves who are gift, and so are called upon (as creatures aware of that fact) to return all that we are to the giver. Hence the insistence in Islam that the goal of human life consists in the ongoing practical recognition that God is Lord of all, while the elaborate structure of the entire second part of the *Summa Theologiae* of Aquinas is designed to show how we can return our whole selves to the One who is our source.

Ghazali seems to put the heart (with its array of desires) first in his anthropology, while Aquinas stresses the role of intellect and of understanding. However, intellect is ever for Aquinas at the service of this inner imperative of *return;* the very structure of the *Summa* itself displays what is for him the existential context of human understanding. But such a requirement to return all that we are to the One from whom we derive could easily be parsed as total submission, which is also usually offered as a translation of 'Islam'. If that is the case, how can either tradition speak of friendship with this creator-God, much less make of it the apogee of the human-divine relationship? Or, recalling Aristotle's objection to the very possibility of friendship with divinity, what happens once divinity has been removed from the universe itself, and we are faced with an "infinite qualitative difference" (as Kierkegaard phrased it) between creator and all creatures, including intentional ones? Friendship demands reciprocity, and both of these implications of the doctrine of creation emphatically rule that out. Or so it seems. Yet the same revelation which introduces the arresting assertion of free creation also asserts (in the Qur'an): "God will bring a people whom He loves and who love Him" (5:54), and "God loves those who turn unto Him" (2:222). The Hebrew prophets resonate with such language: "I shall betroth you to myself for ever . . . in uprightness and justice, and faithful love (*hesed*) and tenderness" (Hos 2:21), and Jesus himself says to his disciples on the eve of his death: "I shall no longer call you servants; . . . I call you friends" (Jn 15:15). Moreover, both traditions, biblical and Qur'anic, acknowledge Abraham to have been chosen and called "friend" by God. The implication seems to be that the same initiative which created "the heavens and the earth and all that is between them" (that is, us) can also see to it that we are constituted in a reciprocal relationship with our creator.

The theologically minded can detect here the impulse to secure a supernatural status for those creatures offered a reciprocal relationship with their creator, for otherwise it would be quite impossible for them to effect a commensurate response.[6] That was indeed Aquinas' strategy, as we shall see, while Ghazali's is less clearly articulated. What remains true for both, however, is the grounding fact that the divine initiative makes reciprocity possible, much as the Hebrew scriptures insist that the covenantal relationship is founded on the gift of Torah. Indeed, it will be illustrative to watch each of our thinkers negotiate this Scylla and Charybdis, for the Hebrew picture seems to structure their discussion, even though covenant itself remains a background notion for each. Aquinas' treatment is cast explicitly in the Aristotelian anthropology, which his age found so exciting, of passions (or desire) and virtues, to which he adds a third level: gifts of the Spirit.[7] Ghazali, at least in the *Ihyâ'*, relies on the anthropology at work among Sufis, according to which human beings can become increasingly responsive to the providential action of God at work in the world, and through that very response allow the activity of the creator greater and greater sway in their lives, so that they may, in the stage of intimacy with God [*uns*], "act with the very action of God" (*AD* 263). This latter phrase will characterize human actions, inspired by the gifts of the Spirit, in Aquinas' third level. Thus discrepancy in anthropologies may not entail significant differences in describing the stages in this relationship of creatures to creator, a relationship whose paradigm lies in the way in which friendship elicits a synchronicity in friends' pursuits.

## 2. Aquinas' Scheme: Passions, Virtues, Gifts of the Spirit

What is remarkable in reading Aquinas today is the way in which we are able to acknowledge his sources in scripture, underscored in the opening question of the *Summa* and detailed in his commentaries on diverse books of the Old and New Testaments. This treasure had been virtually ignored by Thomists, anxious to celebrate their mentor's philosophical acumen, and was also minimized by Aquinas himself in the structure and execution of his best-known work, *Summa Theologiae.*[8] We need to see how he puts Aristotle to work in explicating Jesus' words in his final discourse to his disciples: "I call you not servants but friends" (Jn 15:15). Aristotle noted three characteristics of authentic friendship: those who wish well to each other, a genuine reciprocity, and a shared good. Moreover, Aristotle's anthropology of passions and virtues offered a serendipitous groundwork for Aquinas' elaboration of the dynamics of human beings' responding to such an invitation. For the hunger of the heart for what is good lies at the basis of what it is to be a human being for Aristotle, a view inherited from Plato. The more transcendent that good, the more need we have for reason to discern for us the path to take to arrive there, since we are invariably presented with many contenders. This fact introduces choice, while the roots of human freedom lie in the hunger itself.

The hunger of the heart for what is good is evidenced for Aristotle in the passions, a view which Aquinas adopts wholeheartedly.[9] Wayward as they may be, the passions are the root of all activity for an end in human beings, whose task is to channel them to activity which will carry us to authentic rather than illusory goods. That task is entrusted to reason but executed by the virtues which deliberate actions can develop in us. And the role of virtue is to allow our native passions an expression which permits us to do the right thing in the right way at the right time, with an alacrity and spontaneity befitting one whose heart hungers for what is good. Yet since the passions possess a natural order, following that of the constitution of the self imaged in Plato's *Phaedrus*, the virtues will be ordered as well, with temperateness, for example, at the service of courage generally, even though in certain situations we may need to call upon courage to assist us in moderating food, drink, or sex. The ease with which we will be able to call upon virtues to assist each other, however, depends on their being properly ordered and so available. Here is where Aquinas sees God's promise of friendship, made effective in and through Jesus' words, offering a fresh focus to Aristotle's insistence that the virtues be ordered. Much as Plato saw justice as consisting in the harmony of the three virtues which direct the three parts of the self, namely, prudence, courage, and temperateness, so Aquinas saw God's love for us evidenced in the promise of friendship, through the gift of charity, as offering a new ordering for all the other virtues to make one's life a wholehearted response to the creator's invitation (*ST* 2-2.23.8).

This ordering is made possible by a gift which becomes an immanent disposition, as the virtues must be in order to facilitate action. That gift is the theological virtue of charity, which empowers us to respond to Jesus' invitation. It is a created participation in God's love which, orienting us to the source of all existence, thereby orders all our other dispositions to become responses to that same invitation, since "each instance of [its] activity expresses the ruling interest of the will" (Wadell 106, cf. *ST* 1-2.12.2). This account offers a fresh focus to Aristotle's account of character, the complex of virtues available to persons and exhibited in their *characteristic* ways of acting. It also assures that creatures and creator share in the same good, which in this case is the loving activity of the creator, and by virtue of that sharing, allows human creatures to reciprocate by returning that creator's love, thus making friendship possible between such radically disparate beings. So the story usually goes, yet there is a further step in Aquinas, which completes Aristotle's picture of a friend being present to and indeed shaping the very relation by which one relates to oneself.

That relation, in one rendition of the Christian trinitarian conception of God, is the Holy Spirit. The complex of virtues which facilitates our wholehearted response to the creator of all strains towards a kind of "connaturality" with that divine activity, whereby we would be acting by the very activity of God. If we were not created agents to begin with, this final stage would seem to be *ecstatic* in an alienating sense of the term: carrying us out of ourselves so that it is no longer we who act. Yet as created agents, already aware of God as the source of our being, it completes the circle to full possession of that being if we allow God to be what God indeed is: the principle of all our activities. If the disposition to love God above all things, which is the created gift of charity, allows us so to relate to God, the gifts of the Holy Spirit indicate how one so related can act. That is, we act as so-related, and are thereby present to the very relation by which God relates to God's own self, which is the Holy Spirit.[10]

We cannot shape that uncreated relation, it is true, but so acting can certainly shape our relation to ourselves, disposing us perfectly to fulfill the desires of our friend as the way of becoming more truly who it is we are called to become. In this way, the manner of acting which Aquinas dubs "the gifts of the Spirit" is the perfection of the love of friendship in us. These "gifts of the Spirit" do not replace our will so much as they manifest that harmony of wills to which friendship aspires. And since the one from whom we take our cue is the very Love of God, to respond to which is the goal inscribed in our very nature, we are in no danger of alienation by allowing the Spirit to execute that response in us. As Wadell summarizes this final stage, "the paradox of Aquinas' account of the virtues is unflinching: our greatest moral possibility is not to act, but to let ourselves be acted upon by God, for it is when we suffer the divine love that we become most like it" (132). That is what it is to be moved by the Spirit, whose gifts complete the empowerment of the infused virtue of charity by allowing us to be empowered by the personal power and love of God.

While it is true that Aquinas can exploit Aristotle's anthropology of the virtues in a quite specific way, given the Christian doctrine of a triune and incarnate God, we shall see that al-Ghazali presents a remarkably parallel account, although with far less immediate reliance on Aristotle and little or no ontological infrastructure. What does link the two, however, is a robust account of the free creation of the universe, attributable to God alone, without intermediaries of any sort: an untrammeled initiative on the part of the One from whom all that is comes forth, to which all human beings have been invited to respond by the gracious gift of God's own word. For Aquinas that Word was made flesh in Jesus, while for Ghazali it offers a "straight path" in the Qur'an given to Muhammad to recite. Yet that same Qur'an, heard and recollected, will also empower us to respond in a way befitting the gift, as we shall see.

### 3. Ghazali's Pattern

For Ghazali, human love for God (desire) is transformed by God's love for us, leading to intimacy with God [*uns*] and perfect contentment [*ridâ*]: the state of friendship [*wilâya*], in which the creature acts freely with the very freedom of the creator. Aristotle's dynamic of passion and virtue is at best implicit in Ghazali, if present at all. What is central in his anthropology is the heart, with its desires. The heart recognizes the voice of its creator in the recitation of the Qur'an, and the heart responds to that voice, albeit erratically.[11] The discipline which the heart needs is found in the same recitation, whose verses point to and constitute a "straight path." The ninety-nine names of God, culled from the Qur'an, constitute a pattern to which faithful servants of God are called to conform their lives, imitating as best they can the One from whom their existence and activity derives.[12] Ghazali need not contend with a list of human perfections taken over from Hellenic thought, whose ordering would need to be transformed in the light of divine revelation. He begins rather with what Kierkegaard called "the infinite qualitative difference"—the distinction of creature from creator—and proceeds to delineate how human beings may be led, by the Qur'an, to traverse that chasm by a journey leading to "intimacy with God."[13]

The guides on this journey are largely Sufi masters, who identify the stations along the way and display by their lives the
transformations possible to human beings who set out reso-
lutely on this path. Without having recourse to anything so explicit as a "supernatural elevation," Ghazali nonetheless presupposes that God's love can bring creatures to a greater and greater
proximity to the creator. The point of encounter is the human
heart, and the divine action is invariably described as "removing
the veil from one's heart, in order that one can see with one's
heart, to be elevated to God's own self along with those who are
already near to God" (*LA* 156). The progressive stations are then
described as successive unveilings of the heart, and the dynamic
is summarized as follows: "In this way the love of God for His
servants brings them closer to Himself, removing their negli-
gences and sins from them by purifying their inner self (*bâtin*)
from the filth of this world. God removes the veil from their
hearts, in such a way as they contemplate what they see in their
hearts" (*LA* 159). He proceeds to distinguish this transforming
love of God from the servants' response, which consists in "the
desire which animates them to seize hold of the perfection
which they lack" (*LA* 159). There lies the lack of symmetry in the
two loves: while God's is transforming, ours seeks transformation; yet the dynamic of "the way" is to bring us to the point
where our response is a perfect reflection of God's initiating
love: "the one who has entered into intimacy with God is one
who acts with the very action of God" (*AD* 263).

But in what does such intimacy consist, and would one be
correct to assimilate it to friendship? To be sure, Ghazali has no
Aristotelian analysis to rest his account upon, yet his assemblage
of living examples from a vast repertory of Sufi masters displays

people who live in a kind of exchange with God quite similar to Aristotle's account of friendship. Indeed, that must be what makes the stories so attractive. Since this exchange takes place within, one needs signs which will discern the genuine article from ever-present pretensions. Signs that God loves a person begin with the paradoxical one that the person is subjected to trials (*LA* 160), which is complemented by the assurance that God cares for such persons, taking charge of their external affairs as well as their inner life (*LA* 160). Signs that one responds to that love are generally more conventional in nature, and can be summarized as showing that one loves God above all other things (*LA* 163–206), yet all the while "keeping that love hidden and refraining from proclaiming or otherwise manifesting one's joy" (*LA* 198).

The accounts which inform Ghazali's treatment are characterized by an utter assurance that the person is loved and cared for, and so treated by God as God's friend, even though the dimension of trials reminds us of Teresa of Avila's celebrated retort that if that was how God treated his friends, it was no wonder he had so few of them! Moreover, Ghazali is scrupulous in avoiding any hint of the propensity of some Sufis towards "annihilation [*fanâ*]" in God, which could only conceive of broaching the given "infinite qualitative difference" by dissolving it and thus absorbing the human protagonist into the divine unity. He does insist that the linchpin of Islam, faith in divine unity [*tawhîd*], entails that none truly exist but God, by whose existence all else exists. Those who have reached the stage of intimacy with God appreciate that grounding fact better than most, and so realize that "they act with the very action of God" (*AD* 263). Indeed, "servants of this sort are no longer aware of existing on their own" (*AD* 263), and so can be said to be "annihilated [*fanya*] in the oneness of God," but only in the carefully de-lineated sense of "the loss of awareness of oneself as an au-tonomous agent" (*AD* 262).[14]

Marie-Louise Siauve finds that "such intimacy is no longer 'with God' but 'in God'; God acts in the person and by the per-son. Those who are intimates of God are no longer aware of ex-isting by themselves, but only of being servants of God" (*AD* 263). This state is certainly comparable to Aquinas' final stage of acting by the Spirit and being moved by the gifts of the Spirit. For Siauve, this culminating state offers a key to the unity of Ghazali's thought: "God is one, omnipresent and the only [full-fledged] agent in creation. Those who are intimates of God's not only progress indefinitely, by the élan of his love, towards an ever greater intimacy with God, but if they should attain God, their encounter [*wajd*] with God allows them to live in intimacy with God, taking joy in what gives joy to God, acting with the very action of God. They become aware of neither existing nor acting except by the act by which God gives them existence and movement. One could then say of them that they have let them-selves be 'annihilated', in order to be nothing but the act of God in the creature. In their intimacy with God, their hearts are en-larged to the measure of the Generosity of God" (*AD* 267–68).

Ghazali's reliance on the example and stories of Sufi mas-ters allows him to finesse some of the conceptual conundra involved in characterizing a relationship across the "infinite qualitative difference." The full-blooded characters bodied forth in the Sufi stories, however, certainly belie any caricature of the goal of the Sufi path as "existential monism," to register one reading of Ibn Arabi's celebrated "unity of existence [*wahdat al-wujûd*]."[15] What seems to emerge is a lived familiarity which needs to respect "the distinction" in such a way as to grant that however reciprocal things may be, the source of all remains just that, so that the reciprocity is ever a divine gift. Human action for both Aquinas and Ghazali will ever be created action; paradigmatic human initiative will be a response to an invitation freely offered by the One whose free action initiated it all, so that one can say that human creativity will be, at its best, created creativity. That perspective remains an affront—an "offense," Kierkegaard would say—to other conceptions of the *humanum* which trade on "autonomy," but in that offense lies a challenge: which account offers a better rendition of something immensely valuable to all human beings, friendship?

### 4. Conclusion: Parallels, Functional Equivalencies, and Differences between Ghazali and Aquinas

That human beings are destined for friendship with God is hardly the impression which observers have either of Christianity or of Islam, although this development in Christianity might not be found untoward, given that the Word of God was made flesh in Jesus. In Islam, however, where the Word was made Arabic in the Qur'an, the watchword has long been submission to the "straight path" delineated therein, by way of obedience to the law [*shar'ia*] derived from it. The fact that a theologian as central to Islam as al-Ghazali would propose that a reciprocal love between Muslims and the one God offers the paradigm form of Islam challenges those stereotypes and counters the commonplace translation of 'Islam' as 'submission'. And while there is no doubt that his Ash'arite tendencies may have facilitated his manner of articulating the mutuality of divine and human love in this exchange, his anthropology is more clearly derived from the Sufis. It is here that the parallels emerge between his dynamic and that of Aquinas.

What seems crucial is that neither thinker had to secure human dignity in the face of the creator by pure initiative. Both see human action at its best as a response to the divine initiative, and this response-character of human activity as a corollary of the originating creature-creator relationship. Given that structure, and the opening to an interpersonal relationship at the divine initiative, it becomes possible to dare to think that creatures might (adapting Aristotle's culminating word on friends) stand in the same relationship to God as to themselves, and that God, the partner, would stand in the same relationship to a creature as to God's own self! This is indeed the most acceptable formula for an intimacy which not only allows but demands that each be itself, while acknowledging and celebrating that each lives by the life of the other. While Aquinas (and the Christian tradition generally) saw in the very terms of this description a demand for a supernatural status, both to permit reciprocity in the creature-creator interaction and to secure the integrity of the creature's response, Ghazali's reliance on the Sufi notion of *heart* proffers a more continuous path of "drawing near to God," punctuated by discrete stages yet culminating in a freedom bestowed by God to created responders so that their hearts may respond wholeheartedly.

Ontologies apart, however, these seem to be two complementary ways of articulating a paradigmatic way of relating that is available to creatures of a creator who makes the divine initiatives known. In that respect, they stand together against all Pelagian forms of Christianity as well as all forms of Islam which must open and close their presentation with the *shar'ia*. And since variant Pelagian readings of Christianity are arguably dominant, and the same could be said for *shar'ia* Islam, this comparative sketch of two religious thinkers central to each tradition, bringing the mutual illumination it does, may offer some hope for a rapprochement in the face of stereotypes reinforced by majority attitudes. What is more, one may even hope that so careful a delineation of friendship with the creator of all could redound to our understanding and practice of friendship among this same One's servants and friends, so that Aristotle's ideal of friends in "the good" could help us move beyond mutual exploitation to genuine mutuality.

## Notes

1. See my *Knowing the Unknowable God: Ibn-Sina, Maimonides, Aquinas* (Notre Dame, Ind.: University of Notre Dame Press, 1986), and *Freedom and Creation in Three Traditions.*

2. See also Genesis 18:17, Wisdom 7:27, Isaiah 41:8, 2 Chronicles 20:7.

3. Paul Wadell, *Friends of God* (New York: Peter Lang, 1991); M. L. Siauve, *L'amour de Dieu chez Gazâlî* (Paris: Vrin, 1986) = *AD*, and *Livre de l'amour,* introduction, traduction et notes par M. L. Siauve (Paris: Vrin, 1986) = *LA*. Wadell's earlier work, *Friendship and the Moral Life* (Notre Dame, Ind.: University of Notre Dame Press, 1989), offers a more comprehensive picture of friendship and ethics. A series of essays edited by Oliver Leaman, *Friendship East and West: Philosophical Perspectives* (London: Curzon, 1996), offers a wide spectrum of views from diverse religious traditions.

4. Thomas Hanley, "St. Thomas' Use of Al-Ghazali's *Maqasid-al-falasifa,*" *Medieval Studies* 44 (1982): 243–70.

5. Richard Gramlich, *Muhammad al-Gazzâlîs Lehre von den Stufen zur Gottesliebe* [ = translation of books 31–36 of Ghazali's *Ihyâ' 'Ulûm ad-Dîn*] (Weisbaden: Franz Steiner, 1984), 524.

6. Thomas O'Meara, O.P., "Virtues in the Theology of Thomas Aquinas," *Theological Studies* 58 (1997): 254–85.

7. I am indebted to Wadell for this scheme.

8. Eugene Rogers Jr. has effectively made this point in his *Thomas Aquinas and Barth: Sacred Doctrine and Natural Knowledge of God* (Notre Dame, Ind.: University of Notre Dame Press, 1995).

9. Simon Harak, S.J., *Virtuous Passions: The Formation of Christian Character* (New York: Paulist, 1993).

10. Stanza 38 of the *Spiritual Canticle* of John of the Cross shows how one trained in the thought of Aquinas will put it, speaking of the spouse: "Besides teaching her to love purely, freely, and disinterestedly, as He loves her, God makes her love Him with the very strength with which He loves her. Transforming her into His love, . . . He gives her His own strength by which she can love Him. As if He were to put an instrument in her hands and show her how it works by operating it jointly with her, He shows her how to love and gives her the ability to do so" (*Collected Works of John of the Cross,* trans. Kieran Kavanaugh and Otilio Rodriguez [New York: Doubleday, 1964] 554).

11. See the selections from Ghazali's *Ihyâ' 'Ulûm ad-Dîn* in Richard Joseph McCarthy, S.J., *Freedom and Fulfillment* (Boston: Twayne, 1980), appendix 5, 363–82.

12. *Al-Ghazali on the Ninety-Nine Beautiful Names of God,* trans. David Burrell and Nazih Daher (Cambridge: Islamic Texts Society, 1992).

13. "The distinction" is Robert Sokolowski's key expression in *The God of Faith and Reason;* "infinite qualitative difference" may be found, *inter alia,* in *The Sickness unto Death,* ed. and trans. Howard and

Edna Hong (Princeton, N.J.: Princeton University Press, 1980), 99. For "intimacy with God," see Siauve, *LA*, 207–14; *AD*, 246–68.

14. Ghazali pursues the implications of *tawhîd* [faith in divine unity] for human actions in the book preceding the *Book of Love* in the *Ihyâ' 'Ulûm ad-Dîn*: the *Book of Faith in Divine Unity [tawhîd] and Trust in Divine Providence [tawakkul]*, trans. David Burrell (Louisville, Ky.: Fons Vitae, 2000).

15. To follow the discussion of this key term from Louis Massignon's ground-breaking *Passion of al-Hallaj*, trans. Herbert Mason (Princeton, N.J.: Princeton University Press, 1982), passim, to the recent work of William Chittick, *The Sufi Path of Knowledge* (Albany: State University of New York Press, 1989) and *Imaginal Worlds: Ibn Arabi and the Problem of Religious Diversity* (Albany: State University of New York Press, 1994), is to gain considerably in one's appropriation of Ibn Arabi.

# 5

# *Friendship and Discourse about Divinity*

## Lest God be god

Friends embarked on an intellectual journey can transform a debate into a discussion, because their care for one another is shaped by their attentiveness to the search they share for truth. Once again, friendship requires not agreement but devotion to an ideal—the *good*—which lures us on together. The friends I envisage in this concluding essay are the philosophically inclined and especially those who are self-styled atheists. For as a person of faith, I cherish atheists as conversation partners, yet need them to be authentic atheists. That means, of course, that their denial envisages one who is truly God, and not some residual childhood image or something concocted by philosophers of religion—for denying idols of that sort sheds no light at all on the subject of our inquiry. One of the German theologians courageous enough to stand up to the Nazis, indeed, to lend his support and his life to the plot to assassinate Hitler, Dietrich Bonhoeffer, spoke of the ordeal of Christians under the Third

Reich as moving those who responded beyond conventional Christianity, which he dubbed "cheap grace." Analogously, I should like to encourage atheists beyond a cheap atheism to the genuine article. Yet, as we shall see, to rise to the quality of affirmation needed to locate God properly (over against other objects of knowledge) will require more than careful formulation—though we shall employ a great deal of that. The extra ingredient will be what friends supply to one another in encouraging one another to continue on a path which always threatens to peter out. Let us see how this works out as we seek to be clear what we are affirming or denying when we refer to God.

One might have thought that would be easy enough, just as Europeans find it easy to be "post-Christian" when they are surrounded by splendid cathedrals, but that is precisely why authentic atheism proves so elusive. Allow me two examples. In 1967 an essay appeared by one of my graduate school professors, Russ Hanson, detailing his objections to attempts to prove that God exists.[1] After trotting out the usual responses to the standard "proofs," he outlined one that would convince him. Were he to be walking along the quad (of course!) with students or colleagues, and a large Zeus-like figure appeared in the sky, singling him out with the monition, "Hanson, I've had enough of your logic-chopping; be it known that I exist!", such an event, he averred, would prove convincing. When I read it I was horrified; if the God whom I professed to believe in turned out to be a large Zeus-like figure, I would have felt utterly betrayed. There was an immense miscommunication somewhere. More recently, Daniel Dennett, in his popular presentation, *Darwin's Dangerous Idea,* rhetorically exploits a particular picture of God as creator in order to render Darwin's idea dangerous.[2] We could, no doubt, take issue with his rendition of Darwin's idea, namely, that "an impersonal, robotic, mindless little scrap of molecular machinery is the ultimate basis of all the agency, and hence meaning, and hence consciousness in the universe" (203). His use of the contrasting images of cranes and sky-hooks offers a cumulative picture of the kind of explanatory devices he deems respectable in a scientific inquiry, but the key phrase "ultimate basis" remains ambiguous.[3] He remains fascinated with its import, however, as earlier *obiter dicta* reveal.

Where Darwin needed order plus time to derive design, Dennett notes how his successors will generate order out of randomness and eternity. "What is there left to explain? Some people think there is still one leftover 'why' question: *Why is there something rather than nothing?*" (180). He wonders whether this question is itself intelligible (referring us to Robert Nozick's *Philosophical Explanations,* chapter 2), conceding that "if it [is], the answer 'Because God exists' is probably as good an answer as any, but look at its competition: 'Why not?'" (181). The cavalier quality of this response nicely exemplifies the description he had earlier endorsed, of "philosophical theology as 'intellectual tennis without a net'" (154), yet it is outdone by a later rendition of the vanishing role for intelligent agency in our evolving accounts of the creative process: "What is left is what the process, shuffling through eternity, mindlessly finds (when it finds anything): a timeless Platonic possibility of order. That is indeed a thing of beauty, as mathematicians are forever exclaiming, but it is not itself something intelligent but, wonder of wonders, something intelligible. Being abstract and outside of time, it is nothing with an *initiation* or *origin* in need of explanation. What does need its origin explained is the concrete universe itself, [yet] why not stop at the material world? *It,* we have seen, does perform a version of the ultimate bootstrapping stick; it creates itself *ex nihilo*, or at any rate out of something that is well-nigh indistinguishable from nothing at all. Unlike the puzzling, mysterious, timeless self-creation of God, this self-creation is a non-miraculous stunt that has left lots of traces" (185). (If any student of the medievals who tussled with this question had been invited to string a net for that last game, a few of the dazzling serves would have been caught short: like *ex nihilo* or something much like it, or God's self-creation.)

The point here, however, is not to contest this philosopher's competence to handle questions verging on the "ultimate basis" of the universe but merely to notice his fascination with them; and like Hanson before him, his apparent presumption that he has them right: that he understands the proper terms in which they are to be parsed and can handle them effectively. But if philosophers as astute as these can commit such egregious gaffs in attempting to characterize the creator of all-that-is, what kind of caricatures must many philosophers be working with when such questions arise? This query is best left rhetorical, I am sure, but their ostensible ignorance can find unwitting support in the vague philosophical construct called "theism" which many philosophers of religion seem content to work with. It is notably vague in that much discussion invoking it opposes theists to atheists with little or no reflection of what one is affirming and the other denying. My contention will be that discourse about God needs training, like any discourse. We learn to speak any language in a community of language users, and what we may invoke as "our intuitions" are in fact the shared presumption of that community. I shall further contend that there is no generic "theism" any more than there are generic animals, but that there are ways of approaching God, each of which requires an initial as well as continuing steps of faith. A God proposed as culminating a philosophical system would not answer to the claims of major religious communities regarding the God they worship, and such communities ought to be granted some insight into such matters. Indeed, as we privilege communities of scientific inquirers in matters of science, ought we not privilege religious communities in matters of divinity?

The closest thing to "generic theism" is Plotinus, yet his rendition of all things emanating from "the One" did not pretend to be a purely philosophical account, but entailed a commensurate way of life, a series of exercises reminding its adherents that such an inquiry must involve a personal transformation if it is to reach its goal.[4] That is why Augustine, once he had resolved the philosophical conundra in the way of understanding divinity, saw the step before him involving a choice between Platonism and Christianity (*Confessions*, bk. 7). If the "Platonism" in question were nothing more than a philosophical trajectory, why the forced option? The reason why more than philosophy must be involved goes to the heart of this essay. The God whom the rabbis and the mullahs denote as *One* cannot itself be identifiable as part of a conceptual scheme useful to categorize things in the world, for that would prohibit our identifying it as the "source of all"; logically, the one which is the source of all-that-is cannot belong to that set.[5] Yet we must be able to speak of it; it cannot outstrip all discourse, even though its status places it beyond all-that-is.

The way in which the various traditions have approached this dilemma is by incorporating diverse "spiritual exercises" into their formation, with the goal of orienting our intellectual inquiry beyond its normal ambit in a direction designed to attain something of its object. In this way, they have shown their respect for the role of philosophical discourse—at once positive and negative—while acknowledging its inherent limitations. That role is positive best where its negative role is paramount: identifying incoherent statements, noting that this unique object is *unlike* anything we know, yet all the while respecting an inherent orientation of the intellect to know what is real.[6] To be sure, these traditions found it easier to respect such an orientation when they also averred that our inquiring minds were created "in the image of" their creator, so that the "source of all" became at once the goal of that subset of creatures who were themselves intelligent. Yet that assertion was also deemed to be detectable in the inquiring spirit of our minds, which requires us to seek reasons why, and strains towards complete explanations. The essential point is not that the assertion of a creator will afford anything completely within those parameters, as we have seen, but that the orientation and the demand point beyond what we are able to come up with. (This is to me the most fruitful way to understand the role which "proofs" for God's existence play in thinkers like Aquinas, placed as they are preliminary to theological inquiry.)[7]

Robert Sokolowski uses his phenomenological expertise to sum up this state of affairs regarding discourse about divinity by speaking of "the distinction," indeed, "the Christian distinction."[8] In the spirit of Aquinas, who put commonplace grammatical or semantic distinctions to a new use in making a metaphysical point, Sokolowski reminds us that distinctions are ingredient in our knowing anything at all, since to know something is this involves distinguishing it from that. Furthermore, any inquiry requires distinguishing one's object from misleading surrogates. Yet the distinction of God from the world is quite unlike any other distinction we employ, since we mean thereby to distinguish God from everything else that is, in such a way that God is the source of all-that-is. The upshot of this is multiple, beginning with the realization that the believer's universe does not contain one more item than the unbeliever's. What the believer rather does is to acknowledge the universe to have a unique source, yet a unitary source which cannot be placed over against the universe as though it were on a par with those things in the universe that we need to distinguish from other things in identifying the object of our inquiry.[9] Why not? Because it would then no longer occupy the metaphysical location proper to a creator of all-that-is.

Whoever would distinguish the creator from other things as though it were one item among them, would thereby misapprehend the causality proper to creation by thinking of the creator as in a reciprocal relation to creatures. How must the causality proper to creation be characterized? That the creator is the cause of being of whatever is: the precise point where a religious avowal of God as creator demands a metaphysics which allows one to speak of the *being* of things and so gain some idea of what it might be to be a "cause of being."[10] If one glibly speaks of a creator without even gesturing towards such metaphysical uniqueness, it is inevitable that one will picture God as "the biggest thing around," and the usual competitive scenarios between, say, human and divine freedom will emerge. Sokolowski uses the ubiquitous notion of *distinction* to call attention to this singular distinction whereby one term—the universe—might not even have been, were it not for the free activity of the other. In other words, the very being of anything that exists is dependent on the activity of the creator as its continuing source. Avicenna had adapted the Hellenic notion of *necessary being* to call attention to this situation when he divided *being* into *necessary* and *contingent,* with God alone constituting "necessary being."[11] Yet the necessity involved was no longer Aristotle's sense of "could not be otherwise," but a novel one of "could not not be": God alone exists "by right," as it were, being "necessarily existent in itself," whereas existence "comes to" everything else, even those things which were considered always to have been— "necessary beings" in the Hellenic universe.[12]

Western readers will be reminded of Anselm, of course, and Sokolowski's rendering of "the Christian distinction" offers fresh insight into Anselm's recursive formula—"that than which nothing greater can be thought"—as well as a crucial corrective to recent attempts to enlist Anselm in support of a hybrid called "perfect being theology."[13] Sokolowski contends that the intention of Anselm's formula is to assert that nothing—not even God plus the world—can be greater than God.[14] His interpretation is contestable, of course, though it receives support from other passages in the *Proslogion*. For our purposes, it forcibly calls attention to the recursive character of the celebrated formula, prohibiting a casual reading whereby God would simply be the most perfect of beings. And it also accounts for the easy transition within Anselm's articulated argument from "what cannot be thought not to be" to "what cannot not be," thus allowing him to identify the one arrived at by his "simple argument" with the creator of all revealed in Genesis. For the one whose nature it is simply to be will be able to be the source of being for anything that is.

Now we begin to see why Sokolowski acknowledged that this "distinction is glimpsed on the margin of reason, [indeed] it may be said to be at the intersection of faith and reason" (39). For it does not function like other distinctions, to separate off God from other things; rather, "in the Christian distinction God is understood as 'being' God entirely apart from any relation of otherness to the world or to the whole. God could and would be God even if there were no world. Thus the Christian distinction is appreciated as a distinction that did not have to be, even though it in fact is. [Even more,] the most fundamental thing we come to in Christianity, the distinction between the world and God, is appreciated as not being the most fundamental thing after all, because one of the terms of the distinction, God, is more fundamental than the distinction itself" (32–33). In this sense, "the distinction" is properly inconceivable without first properly conceiving its more fundamental term, God, yet "the distinction" offers the best avenue we have for not misconceiving God as one more item in the universe. So there is a circularity here that is intrinsic to the venture of God-talk, making "the distinction" properly inconceivable, though Sokolowski reminds us that it is operative throughout Christian practice.

Why, then, insist on it? Because otherwise our discourse about God will not be about God but about some substitute, an idol; and idolatry has always been considered worse than atheism among the Abrahamic faiths. Atheism can be accounted to foolishness; idolatry is ever nefarious. Hence my interest in "the distinction": to expose idolatry for what it is, so as to allow self-styled atheists to know what it is they ought properly deny to deserve the name. Otherwise, they will just be foolish, like Hanson and Dennett! An effort to deconstruct much philosophy of religion will offer others the opportunity to construct an authentic atheism: such is my philosophical intent (as well as pastoral purpose). That is also why I prefer to consider this essay as an exercise in "philosophical theology" rather than in "philosophy of religion." That the purported subject is *God* makes it theology, and while the mode is explicitly philosophical, the nature of the subject must guide our inquiry by discerning which categories we find appropriate. By contrast with Descartes' dream of a "universal method," this Aristotelian requirement assures that such an inquiry will have twin criteria: rational cogency plus the categorial discernments attained by a religious tradition.

That means that we will not be able to use ordinary philosophical predilections as *a priori* criteria for adjudicating arguments in this domain. For example, as a quick survey would reveal, most philosophers have an inbuilt preference for univocity in argument, and rightly so, for equivocity undermines the ordinary processes of entailment. So I have found Sokolowski's precisions about "the distinction" a useful starting point, since they prepare one to acknowledge that there is no hope of even attempting to locate divinity without an awareness of the analogical reaches of language. And this rather sophisticated semantic point is detected in practice by the nose which believers develop for discriminating effective preaching from its opposite. There must be something in homilists' use of language which betrays their sense that the words they are using signify at best "imperfectly" what they are trying to say.[15] If they presume that the terms they are using of God are univocal in character, with God exemplifying their outer reach, then the God presented to us will be the "biggest thing around," and "the distinction" will have been elided. It is not that preachers focus on "the distinction," but rather that it should govern the entire span of their discourse. As we shall see, this reflects the relation of questions

3–11 in Aquinas' *Summa Theologiae,* which serve to locate God as the object of inquiry, to question 13, where he discusses which "names" we might use for God and how we should use these terms.

More significantly, as Sokolowski insists, this distinction "receives its formulation in reflective thought because it has already been achieved in the life that goes on before reflective thinking occurs. . . . The Christian distinction between God and the world is there for us now, as something for us to live and as an issue for reflection, because it was brought forward in the life and teaching of Christ, and because that life and teaching continue to be available in the life and teaching of the church. This is how the Christian understanding of God as creator, the understanding that Anselm formulates for us, has been in fact achieved" (23–24). And that is why tradition must afford one set of criteria for discourse in philosophical theology. I would expand the traditions in question to include Jewish and Muslim, and even Vedantic, but comparative issues would only distract us here.[16] The crucial point is to note that this criterion eliminates the strategy employed by so-called "perfect being theology," which "centers on the conception of God as the greatest possible, or maximally perfect, being, an individual who has the greatest possible array of properties it is intrinsically good to have."[17] As we shall see, such a starting point also allows one to generate a neutral "theism," which can then stand in as a philosophical analogue for specific religious traditions.

What "the distinction" reminds us is that God cannot be thought of as "a perfect being" or even as *the* perfect being; that the source of all that is cannot be an individual who instantiates "properties [which we believe] it is intrinsically good to have," since as the creator of all God must be the source of all the perfections that we find, and as their source, "possess" them intrinsically—that is, neither *possess* them nor *instantiate* them, but *be* them.[18] This characterization follows from "the distinction" inasmuch as "God is understood not only to have created the world, but to have permitted this distinction between himself and the world to occur. [Yet since] no distinction made within the horizon of the world is like this, . . . the act of creation cannot be understood in terms of any action or any relationship that exists in the world" (33). The "non-reciprocal relation of dependence" which is creation sets off creator from creature in a way that assures their intimacy as well, since "apart from that relation of total dependence no created being would *be* at all."[19] This characterization of God as creator led Moses Maimonides to insist that there can be no "similarity" or shared meaning between terms attributing features to God and those same terms used of human beings. For what are features in us are not features *of* God, but belong essentially to God as the creator and hence source of all perfections.[20]

In other words, the metaphysical implication (and presupposition) of "the distinction" is divine simpleness, for there is simply no other way to identify the creator uniquely as the subject of inquiry.[21] Any other path would have to distinguish God from anything that is not God by a "divine feature," perhaps identifying these by superlatives of perfections deemed to be so in the human case, as "perfect being theology" does. Yet such a strategy would inescapably presuppose that one could talk about this being along with others, perhaps as the "most perfect" among them, leaving unaddressed the uniqueness of the relation of a free creator to all that is; that is, the relation of God as the "cause of being," or the question of God's own origins. Even if God were asserted to be that being "necessary 'in' all possible worlds," that being's identity as free creator of the universe would have to be separately established. And it is entirely unclear how "necessity" of this sort allows one to think of God without any "world" at all, the very nub of "the distinction" so vital to Jewish, Christian, or Muslim thinking about divinity. Moreover, as Robert Adams avers, the most cogent meaning of "necessary existence" as said of God is that elaborated by Aquinas in identifying this One as the one whose very essence is to exist.[22] And that is the most telling meaning Aquinas gives to divine simpleness.[23]

On this account, then, to say that God simply *is* while everything else *has* being, and has it from God, cannot be a description of God, for we could never know what it was like simply to be. It is rather a statement of what God is *not*, as Aquinas avers in introducing questions 3–11 in the *Summa*. In other words, it reminds us that the creator of all will not be describable in mundane categories, and that those constitute our proper ways of speaking. Yet we cannot be misled by divine simpleness into thinking that this One's lack of complexity of any kind signals an undifferentiated mass. For simpleness in God must constitute perfection, since this One is the source of all that is, and whatever perfections we acknowledge themselves derive from the fact that something exists. Here is where the famous distinction of essence from existing comes in handy. Yet what Aquinas received from Avicenna sounds foreign to us, and it must be admitted that this distinction may only be recognizable in the light of the signal one which has been guiding our inquiry. While it may prove possible to trace a path from the distinction between

essence and existing, recognized in everything which we encounter, to a source of both which transcends all that we know
by lacking that ultimate form of metaphysical composition, the
path may also be the reverse.[24] It may be that we will be guided
to acknowledge such a distinction only after we have been persuaded of the more primal "distinction," thus recognizing that
everything that is receives its very being as a free gift.

Let us recall our initial methodological observations, bringing them to bear on these matters. An account of divinity that is
properly executed in philosophical theology will acknowledge
twin criteria of adequacy. The key metaphysical distinction (between essence and existing) which allows one to give a cogent
account of "the distinction" (of creator from creatures) seems to
occupy a logical neighborhood proximate to that view of the
universe which requires "the distinction." The decision to adopt
that view may be facilitated by philosophical arguments, as well
as motivated by the cumulative effect of other events in our
lives, yet the path to discerning whether the being of things is a
mere given or a free gift has ever been a circuitous one. So long
as we are willing to regard the universe as a given, in the mathematical sense of "given" which presupposes no giver, we can just
as easily regard "existence [as] an on/off property; either you're
there or you're not," invariant from one existent to another.[25]
On such a view, the distinction between essence and existing
amounts to very little, for *existing* is little more than a floor for
anything that is. What could lead one to regard *existing*, with
Aquinas, not as a floor but as a pervasive *act?* For one thing,
the sense that an infant contains within itself the virtualities of its
development, notwithstanding the myriad environmental in-
fluences that will go into shaping it. Are we to regard everything
that we have become as literally *added on* to the "mere being" that

we are, or are we to maintain that the potentiality to become what we have become is indeed part of what it was to be in the first place? In fact, Aquinas' lyricism about *existing* may well find its adequate source in his vision of being as a free gift of the One-who-is. Yet once having adopted that vision, do not its consequences imply things that we find congenial with a view of the universe which respects individuals for what they can become as well as for what they have already achieved? In short, a view of *existence* which sees it as the source of all subsequent virtualities (or real possibilities for the thing in question) seems to be closer to our understanding of things than regarding it simply as a floor, an "on/off property."

Such a mode of argumentation can at best be rhetorical in nature, much like the pattern for "proofs" for God's existence, which customarily take schemes of explanation and show them to be inadequate without postulating something more, yet can never claim that the presence of a divine being offers a more complete explanation in the sense intended. To do so would fly in the face of "the distinction" by proposing divinity as the linchpin in an explanatory scheme. Such "proofs" are simply reminding one that complete explanations are not to be had, and so inviting one to look beyond them.[26] And that is where the creator must subsist: beyond any causal feature or agent with which we are acquainted—another statement of "the distinction." So God as creator of all and divine simpleness are two sides of the same coin. And that coin cannot be coin of our realm; that is, neither predicate purports to *describe* God, though both aspire to locate divinity metaphysically where it properly belongs: in Plotinus' terms, "beyond *being*," as we know beings, and so "distinguished" from any or all of them, yet in no way "separate" since no creature could *be* without the creator's constant sustaining activity, an activity identical with the act of creating. Divine simpleness, then, adequately distinguishes the creator from all that is created yet also accounts for this One's being creator, since as the One whose essence is simply to-be, God's activity *ad extra* will be to cause the being of things.

Yet that is but one side of the activity of creating; the other is registered by Aquinas' easily misread insistence that this One is not "really related to" what it creates.[27] In saying this he means to call attention to the fact that God's creating is an intentional activity of divinity, and not one which inherently relates God to creation in such a way that God could not be God without being creator as well. The temptation to say just that comes from the rich notion of *existing* as source of all perfections which he has been touting. For such a conception links *being* internally with *good,* and thus invites the Neoplatonic axiom that "good by nature diffuses itself."[28] In a pregnant aside to his consideration of divine triunity, Aquinas makes an observation which reinforces our reading of *creation* as properly understood only from a dual perspective of faith and of metaphysical reflection. While reminding the objector that any insight into the nature of God such as that elaborated in the Christian tradition of trinitarian reflection would be inaccessible to human inquiry outside of God's self-revelation in Jesus, he notes that this new perspective helps us to avoid two common misconceptions of creation:

saying that God made all things by His Word excludes the error of those who say that God produced things of necessity. When we say that in Him there is a procession of love, we show that God produced creatures not because He needed them, nor because of any extrinsic reason, but on account of the love of His own goodness. (*Summa Theologiae* 1.32.1.3)

Should a divinity whose very nature is to exist act to cause other things, it will be the cause of their being. Yet actually being such a cause will require intentional or free activity on God's part, since the divine nature is also through and through intentional. Once again, *existing* needs to be taken as the source of all perfections and not merely as an ontological floor.

To complete this account of the internal linkage between simpleness and creating in God as the conceptual correlate of "the distinction" of creator from creation, two corollaries follow. The first reminds us that all divine action comes under the rubric of *creating,* as we have noted with God's conserving in being what God creates. Hence any talk of God's "intervening" in creation will be at once misleading and inappropriate, and normally signals egregious inattention to "the distinction." That is, people who speak that way are unwittingly thinking of God as a cause alongside the universe acting *upon* it. While that need not be the case, attention to instances usually finds that it is. The second rounds out the picture of *simpleness* (as elaborated by Aquinas in questions 4–11 of the first part of the *Summa*) with the "formal features" which elucidate it, notably God's eternity. And since this is often a contested "feature" of divinity, it not only deserves particular attention, but inquiring into it will help to clarify what one means by "simpleness" as well.[29] I describe unchangeableness and eternity as "formal features" and hence not ordinary features, because that is what they are, and it is telling that Aquinas treats them in a separate place from that of "divine names" or attributes more generally. Unlike any other "name" of

God, there is no feature, *eternity*, which we could know otherwise than predicating it of God. As he puts it, God alone is eternal, whereas Socrates as well as a few others are just.

A "formal feature," by contrast with an ordinary feature, does
not pretend to describe the thing in question but rather attempts
to locate it ontologically.[30] While the expression is borrowed
from Wittgenstein, the notion seems clear enough. *Simpleness*
and *eternity* belong together as a way of identifying the subject of
the inquiry, and thereby setting God off from anything else by
setting the parameters for discourse about divinity. They offer
semantic analogues for "the distinction" by showing that whatever is said of God ("divine names") cannot be said of divinity as
it is said of anything else, thereby addressing the key concern
voiced by Moses Maimonides in treating of biblical language
about God. That suggests why Aquinas treated these features
before talking in general about what we tend to call "divine
attributes," so that whatever "names" one might propose for
God must be employed according to the constraints of the formal features of simpleness and eternality. This is particularly
evident in the final article of question 13 ("on naming God"),
where Aquinas asks whether "affirmative propositions [may]
be correctly formed about God?" For those familiar with the
ongoing conversation, his interlocutor is Moses Maimonides,
who had insisted that none could, under pain of idolatry. In
his constructive proposal, Aquinas concurs with all of "Rabbi
Moses'" animadversions, but insists that "when we make propositions about God we do not say that he has any composition,
we understand him to be simple." Yet, as the turn of phrase betrays, this understanding is inescapably negative, since "when
our minds understand the simple things superior to them we
understand them in our own way, that is, on the model of com-

posite things; not that we understand the simple things to be composite, but that composition is involved in our way of understanding them." Having acknowledged that key premise of Maimonides, however, he goes on to conclude: "Thus the fact that our statements about God are composite does not make them false" (1.13.12.3).

What *we* must conclude from this conclusion is that Aquinas is being utterly true to his framing statement for questions 3–11 on "formal features" of divinity, that if we wish to succeed in saying anything about God we shall always be speaking about what God is *not*. The appellations offered in the psalms used by Jews and Christians in prayer will be misused if we presume that they map onto divinity as ordinary statements map onto objects of our experience. And if this seems to place too metaphysical a constraint on Jewish, Christian, or Muslim prayer or preaching, we can recall Sokolowki's observation that "the distinction" is found first in the practice of a faith community and only subsequently articulated by philosophical theologians. So-called "ordinary believers" are quick to discern whether preachers are observing the key "formal features" or not in treating the life of faith, though they would not of course put it that way! Yet the phrase "negative theology" deserves a more precise exposition than it ordinarily receives. The remarks of Simon Tugwell, a British Dominican, may be particularly helpful:

> It is negative theology, properly understood, which validates the apparent paradox that God has no name and yet every name is God's name. If there is, strictly speaking, no adequate way of talking about God, there is also no way of talking about God that is entirely inadequate either. . . . If we take Dionysian negative theology seriously, it frees us from the

various tyrannies that narrow our religious language and practice. Unduly self-confident affirmative theologies take some
ways of talking and some ways of behaving too seriously,
and deprive the rest of any significance. But it is surely trivial
gods who make most of life trivial.[31]

Beyond assuring one that one has avoided idolatry by not
confusing God with one of God's creatures, however, we need
some assurance that we have gotten divinity right by pointing,
at least, in the right direction. What has been said about the
centrality of *existing,* as well as about existing as the source of all
perfections, offers the pointers we need, and also suggests how
a metaphysics that highlights that element of beings and of
being can work to elucidate the all-important "distinction" as it
is shared by Jews, Christians, and Muslims alike. Some further
collateral advantages of this form of "negative theology" can be
found in two crucial corollaries. The first regards the thorny
questions surrounding divine and human freedom. On our
view, which is that of Aquinas and of a rich tradition, there can
be no competition between these two actors when one is creator
and the other a creature.[32] If God were but "the supreme being"
(in the sense of "the biggest thing around"), such a one would
constantly be in contention with other beings, and tend to "use
up all the air in the universe." It would be inappropriate to begin
to canvass this issue here, as I have done *in extenso* elsewhere, so
suffice it to note how little concerned is Aquinas about the creator's ability to "move the will freely," that is, without in any
way constraining it or derogating from human freedom.[33] That
must be because he perceives clearly that the way in which the
creator *moves* things is quite unlike any other causal influence.

Furthermore, a metaphysics which reinforces "the distinction" in the ways indicated opens us to the mystical, precisely by insisting that God is not alongside or over against the universe. And when "the distinction" shades into "non-duality," we are placed in a favorable position to find mutual illumination in interaction with other religious traditions.[34] Given the hermeneutical and epistemological presumptions of this inquiry—that talk about divinity must inescapably be anchored in a living religious tradition—the possibility of mutual illumination is a prime desideratum. And like those presumptions, it also marks a clear sign of the intellectual and spiritual environment in which we currently live. That is, discussion of issues in philosophical theology will need to rely as much on the clarifications gained by reflection within religious traditions as on more neutral philosophical criteria of logical consistency. For there is a fund of grammatical expertise which comes from operating within a living religious tradition which those who would assess its findings philosophically cannot blithely overlook. Moreover, to remind ourselves that the warp and woof of a faith-tradition is constituted by the cross-hatching of vital friendships helps us to appreciate how faith can become a mode of knowing. Rather than impede critical assessment, it is precisely the shared commitment to seek what is true—especially in matters so arcane as God—that accentuates the need for critical reflection.

## Notes

1. Norwood Russell Hanson, "What I Don't Believe," *Continuum* 5 (1967): 89–105. His comments confirm my point: "Please do not

dismiss this example as a playful, irreverent Disney-oid contrivance. The conceptual point is that *if* such a remarkable event were to transpire, *I* for one should certainly be convinced that God does exist" (93).

2. *Darwin's Dangerous Idea* (New York: Simon and Schuster, 1995).

3. Dennett's statement of faith is given on page 341, where he insists that "like life itself, and every other wonderful thing, culture must have a Darwinian origin. It, too, must grow out of something less. . . , this all has to be built up from scratch. . . . Settling for anything less in the way of an explanation would be just giving up."

4. See Pierre Hadot's *Exercises spirituels et philosophie antique* (Paris: Etudes Augustiniennes, 1987), amplified in an English translation by Michael Chase: *Philosophy as a Way of Life* (Oxford: Blackwell, 1995); as well as Hadot's *Plotinus, or, The Simplicity of Vision.*

5. This is Aquinas' designator of the object of the *Summa* at the outset of the *Summa Theologiae* 1.2.Prol.; as had been remarked, this sounds like Kant *avant la lettre!*

6. In the prologue to his formal treatment of God in the *Summa,* Aquinas says: "Having recognized that a certain thing exists, we have still to investigate the way in which it exists, that we may come to understand what it is that exists. Now we cannot know what God is, but only what he is not; we must therefore consider the ways in which God does not exist, rather than the ways in which he does." (1.3.Prol). On comparing this with the position of Moses Maimonides, see Alexander Broadie, "Maimonides and Aquinas on the Names of God," *Religious Studies* 23 (1987): 157–70.

7. See my "Philosophy and Religion: Attention to Language and the Role of Reason," *International Journal of Philosophy of Religion* 38 (1995): 109–25.

8. *The God of Faith and Reason,* chaps. 3–4.

9. For these rules regarding coherent discourse about divinity, see Kathryn Tanner, *God and Creation in Christian Theology* (Oxford: Blackwell, 1988), chap. 2.

10. For an elaboration of this requirement, see James Ross, "Creation II," in *Existence and Nature of God,* ed. Alfred Freddoso (Notre Dame, Ind.: University of Notre Dame Press, l983), 115–41.

11. See my "Essence and Existence: Avicenna and Greek Philosophy," *Mélanges Institut Dominicain d'Etudes Orientales* (Cairo) 17 (1986): 53–66.

12. See Avicenna's *al-Shifa' (al-Illahiyyat)* bk. 1, chaps. 6–7; French translation by Georges Anawati: *La Métaphysique du Shifa'* (Paris: Vrin, 1978), 106–17.

13. A representative statement of this position may be found in Thomas Morris, "Metaphysical Dependence, Independence, and Perfection," in *Being and Goodness,* ed. Scott MacDonald (Ithaca, N.Y.: Cornell University Press, 1991), 278–97. For an incisive refutation, see Barry Miller, *A Most Unlikely God* (Notre Dame, Ind.: University of Notre Dame Press, 1996).

14. *The God of Faith and Reason,* chap. 1.

15. See Herbert McCabe's appendix to volume 3 of the Blackfriars edition of the *Summa* (London: Eyre and Spottiswoode, 1964): "Signifying Imperfectly."

16. Sokolowski himself acknowledges that "the distinction is lived in Christian life, and most originally it was lived and expressed in the life of Jesus, after having been anticipated, and hence to some extent possessed, in the Old Testament history which Jesus completed" (23). I have essayed interfaith extensions in my "The Christian Distinction Celebrated and Expanded," in *The Truthful and the Good: Essays in Honor of Robert Sokolowski,* ed. James Hart and John Drummond (Dordrecht: Kluwer, 1996). See Sara Grant (note 19).

17. Thomas Morris, "Metaphysical Dependence, Independence, and Perfection," in *Being and Goodness,* ed. MacDonald, 278–97, citation at 278.

18. See Barry Miller's *A Most Unlikely God* (note 13).

19. The quotation is from Sara Grant's Teape lectures: *Towards an Alternative Theology: Confessions of a Non-Dualist Christian* (Bangalore India: Asian Trading Corporation, 1991), which offers a sustained comparative study of Aquinas and Sankar.

20. *Guide of the Perplexed,* II, 50–61; see Broadie (note 6).

21. Brian Davies traces divine *simpleness* to the assertion of God as creator of all-that-is, in "Classical Theism and the Doctrine of Divine Simplicity," in *Language, Meaning and God,* ed. Brian Davies (London: Geoffrey Chapman, 1987), 51–74.

22. I cite Adams as a witness rather than a corroborator, since his expression, "the Thomistic view that God's existence follows necessarily from his essence," does not accurately reflect Aquinas' *identification* of essence with existing in divinity, but it at least attests to the approach: "Divine Necessity," in *The Virtue of Faith* (New York: Oxford, 1987), 209–20, citation at 209. For a critique, see Brian Davies (note 21).

23. See my *Aquinas: God and Action* (Notre Dame, Ind.: University of Notre Dame Press, 1979), chap. 2, noting how *Summa Theologiae* 1.3.4: "Can one distinguish in God essence and existing?" is the centerpiece of question 3, "On God's simpleness."

24. Barry Miller traces the first route in his *From Existence to God* (London: Routledge, 1993).

25. Christopher Hughes, *On a Complex Theory of a Simple God* (Ithaca, N.Y.: Cornell University Press, 1989), 27, where the author states this as a self-evident truth, proceeding to find everything Aquinas has to say in questions 3–11 "unintelligible."

26. See my article cited at note 7.

27. *Summa Theologiae* 1.13.7; see my commentary in *Aquinas: God and Action* (note 23), chap. 6.

28. See Norman Kretzmann, "A General Problem of Creation: Why Would God Create Anything at All?" in *Being and Goodness,* zed. MacDonald, 208–28; and my response in *Freedom and Creation in Three Traditions,* 164–66.

29. I am summarizing the extended treatment in *Aquinas: God and Action* (note 23), chap. 2. See also Thomas Weinandy, O.F.M.Cap., *Does God Change?* (Still River, Mass.: St. Bede's Publication, 1983).

30. See Eddy Zemach, "Wittgenstein's Philosophy of the Mystical," *Review of Metaphysics* 18 (1964): 38–57; reprinted in *Essays on Wittgenstein's Tractatus,* ed. I. M. Copi and R. W. Beard (New York: MacMillan, 1966).

31. *Albert and Thomas: Selected Writings,* translated, edited, and introduced by Simon Tugwell, O.P. (New York: Paulist, 1988), 93.

32. Robert Barron's *Thomas Aquinas: Spiritual Master* (New York: Crossroads, 1995) addresses this in admirably short compass.

33. See my *Freedom and Creation in Three Traditions* chap. 7, for an extended treatment and for the relevant citations from Aquinas.

34. Sara Grant's Teape lectures (note 19) provide a prescient starting point for comparative reflections; I owe the serendipitous phrase "mutual illumination" to my colleague Bradley Malkovsky.

# Index

# About the Author

David Burrell, C.S.C., is currently Theodore Hesburgh Professor in Philosophy and Theology at the University of Notre Dame. He is the author of *Knowing the Unknowable God: Ibn-Sina, Maimonides, Aquinas* (Notre Dame Press, 1986) and *Freedom and Creation in Three Traditions* (Notre Dame Press, 1993). He has been asked to direct the University's Jerusalem program, housed at the Tantur Ecumenical Institute, each spring until 2004.